Patent
Searching

Tools &
Techniques

DAVID HUNT
LONG NGUYEN
MATTHEW RODGERS

1807
WILEY
2007

John Wiley & Sons, Inc.

Library of Congress Cataloging-in-Publication Data:

Hunt, David.
    Patent searching : tools & techniques / David Hunt.
        p. cm.
    Includes index.
    ISBN: 978-0-471-78379-4 (cloth : alk. paper)
1. Patent searching. 2. Patent literature. I. Title. II. Title: Patent searching tools and techniques.
    T210.H86 2007
    025.06'608
                                                        2006030758

10 9 8 7 6 5 4 3 2 1

Contents

About the Editors

David Hunt is the CEO and owner of Landon IP, Inc. He holds a BA and an MBA from the College of William & Mary and has worked as a senior manager in corporate strategy, market research, and competitive intelligence at the Federal Home Loan Mortgage Corporation (Freddie Mac) in McLean, Virginia. Mr. Hunt has served as a project manager at large and small companies in the information technology areas. He has considerable experience in operations management. Mr. Hunt is a member of PIUG and PATMG, which are the professional patent information users groups in the United States and England. He is a member of the International Trademark Association (INTA) as well as the Society for Competitive Intelligence Professionals (SCIP).

Long B. Nguyen is the director of patent search quality for Landon IP, Inc. He holds an MS in engineering management from George Washington University, and a BS in mechanical engineering and a BA in economics from Syracuse University. Mr. Nguyen is a registered patent agent (No. 56,138) with several years of experience in patent prosecution at the United States Patent and Trademark Office (USPTO). While at the USPTO as a patent examiner, he examined technologies that included traction devices, wheels and axles, and tire inflation systems. Mr. Nguyen also has experience in business methods.

Matthew Rodgers is the vice president of the Patent Search Group for Landon IP, Inc. He holds a BS in mechanical engineering from the University of Texas at Austin. Mr. Rodgers has conducted research in semiconductor heat treatment and selective laser sintering. Additionally, he possesses significant experience in the analysis of metallurgical failure. Prior to joining Landon IP, Mr. Rodgers worked for several years as a patent examiner at the USPTO and as a technical specialist who conducted patent searches at other commercial patent search firms. He is a regular faculty member of the leading patent law training company, Patent Resources Group, Inc., of Charlottesville, Virginia.

About Landon IP, Inc.

Landon IP has a long and rich history in the retrieval and analysis of patent and trademark information dating back to 1949. The current company is the consolidation of four separate firms: Cantwell & Paxton (founded in 1949), Betty Byrd Inc. (founded in 1960), Landon & Stark Associates (founded in 1986), and Myra Hunter & Company.

Landon IP conducts professional patent searches for the legal and business communities. The company also analyzes patents and scientific articles, conducts technical intelligence, and consults to corporations and law firms worldwide. Landon IP's information group sells patents, file histories, and other documents on paper and in electronic formats.

The company's primary services include:

- Patent searches that are commissioned by patent attorneys as they counsel clients on patentability, infringement, freedom to operate, state of the art, and validity.

- Complex patent analysis to support research and development, patent valuations, and better licensing decisions.

- Comprehensive federal, state, and common-law trademark searches that identify trademark opportunities in the United States and abroad.

- Patent file histories that are available on paper and electronically by e-mail, CD-ROM, and on the Web.

- Technical translations that are conducted by language and technical specialists with expertise in all major languages and all technical areas.

- Patent application drafting on behalf of companies and law firms in the electrical, mechanical, and biotechnology fields. The company's patent agents do not prosecute applications, but support research scientists and attorneys with professionally drafted invention disclosures, applications, and amendments on a project basis.

Landon IP is one of only two companies awarded the Patent Cooperation Treaty (PCT) patent search pilot contract by the U.S. Patent & Trademark Office (USPTO) in 2005. Landon IP successfully conducted PCT searches for the USPTO in the mechanical, electrical communications, and medical device fields. In 2006, the USPTO awarded Landon IP with a five-year contract to search (PCT) applications in the mechanical, electrical communications, medical device (a.k.a. life sciences), and physical sciences fields.

Acknowledgments

The editors wish to thank the distinguished individuals from both Landon IP, Inc. and Patent Resources Group, Inc. who contributed to this text. This work truly was a team effort and would not have been possible without their efforts.

The opening chapter was written by Sally Sakelaris and Bill Bohlayer, two extraordinary patent information scientists who both specialize in biochemistry. Sally is the Director of Patent Analysis at Landon IP and a faculty member at Patent Resources Group. She has the added distinction of formerly serving as a patent examiner with the USPTO. Bill Bohlayer is an accomplished academic who has been published in biochemistry journals. He is a veteran patent analyst who has conducted searches for companies, patent attorneys, and the USPTO.

Chapter 2, "Types of Patent Searches," was largely written by Matt Meyer, a PhD and team leader of the chemistry and biochemistry groups of Landon IP. Matt is the longest-serving patent analyst on staff with the company, a veteran scientific advisor, and excellent trainer.

Bill Bohlayer, Jamshid Goshtasbi, Benjamin Hitt, Matt Meyer, Blaise Mouttet, Long Nguyen, Dave Odland, Matt Rodgers, and Geoff Thomas drafted Chapter 3, "The Mechanics of Searching." Jamshid, Blaise, and Dave are invaluable analysts in the electrical and physical sciences areas. All three are former USPTO examiners, exceptional communicators, and technical experts. Geoff Thomas is the Director of Patent Searching at Landon IP, has many years of search experience at several organizations and law firms, in a wide variety of subject areas, and was the author of the section on searching foreign patent documents. Ben Hitt and Long Nguyen are primarily mechanical and business methods analysts and both drafted significant portions of the book. Ben was the primary author of Chapter 6, "Search Tools," and contributed to Chapter 3. Long is the director of patent search quality at Landon IP and the primary content editor for the text. As a former USPTO examiner and patent analyst, few individuals know as much about the field of searching as Long. Matt Rodgers is the vice president of the Patent Search Group at Landon IP, a former patent examiner, a former searcher at several organizations, and a veteran faculty member at Patent Resources Group. Without his leadership, this project would not have succeeded.

Robert Cantrell is a thought leader in the gathering, assessment, and communication of patent information for competitive intelligence. He is the author of several books on business strategy and a frequent contributor to intellectual property publications. Robert led the writing on Chapter 4, "Patent Analysis." He is Director of Consulting with Landon IP and a faculty member at advanced programs held by Patent Resources Group. He is a frequent instructor at the U.S. Army War College.

Kristin Hehe is a chemist, search manager, and former patent analyst with exceptional thinking and writing skills. She teamed with Robert Cantrell in drafting Chapter 5, "Approaches to Reporting Search Results." A patent search company cannot succeed without professional search managers who understand the discipline, assess the scope of projects quickly and accurately, and communicate well to individuals who commission the searches. Kristin handles each of those roles exceptionally well.

Ben Hitt and Sally Sakelaris drafted Chapter 6, "Search Tools." You already know their background and contributions. We are very grateful that they readily share their knowledge, skills, and professionalism inside and outside of Landon IP.

Finally, we wish to thank Laurie Baber, Debi Dandridge, and Susan Mathis at Patent Resources Group in Charlottesville, Virginia. Laurie is a professional librarian and provided exceptional support with the facts and diagrams in the text. Debi edited the text for both content and style. Her suggestions were thorough and incorporated in the final manuscript. As with every staff member at Patent Resources Group, Debi is a consummate professional. Susan is an exceptional technical editor, among her other duties. Thank you all.

We hope that you will enjoy reading and referring to the content in this text. As is everything in life, we view the book as a continual work in progress and welcome any suggestions as we improve on these concepts and tools in the future.

David Hunt, CEO
Matt Rodgers, Vice President
Patent Search Group
Long Nguyen, Director
Patent Search Quality
January 1, 2007
Landon IP, Inc.
Alexandria, Virginia USA

Preface

This book on patent searching is the result of a journey. Several years ago, Landon IP was approached by many of our patent attorney customers and asked to conduct prior art searches. Unfortunately, we did not employ any patent searchers, nor did we conduct searches. We were a company that specialized in providing patent information to attorneys and agents since 1949. Patent information, not patent searching, was our business. However, we were determined to learn as much about searching as possible.

My background is in business management. I am not qualified to conduct a patent search. I have an MBA, which means that I can do anything with the help of others and nothing by myself. The fact that I was not a patent searcher told me that I needed to find experts.

So, the company began hiring some very good patent searchers and soon discovered that every one of them learned how to search "on the job"; meaning at the foot of a patent attorney, a patent agent, a librarian, or by themselves. This seemed unusual to us if only because we presumed that so much of the quality and enforceability of a patent depended on the initial patentability search. After all, how many times have you heard the expression "garbage in, garbage out"? Certainly there were many accomplished patent attorneys and exceptional patented technologies. Thousands of attorneys and agents were (and still are) registered to practice before the U.S. Patent and Trademark Office (USPTO) and other patent authorities for that matter. Was there a formal training program for patent searching anywhere?

Well, we quickly learned that no formal search program existed beyond one in the Netherlands and at a few major companies that trained their own people. There were very few books or materials on patent searching.

A text that focused more on tools than timeless principles had been written by a university librarian in Pennsylvania. The Franklin Pierce Law Center also had disseminated some materials, but not a definitive text.

As we became convinced of the need for quality materials and a training program, we contacted Professor Irving Kayton of Patent Resources Group (PRG) in Charlottesville, Virginia. Professor Kayton is a legend in the patent community and conducts highly successful patent bar review and advanced patent law education programs. We asked him whether PRG taught patent search training and, if not, whether he would consider offering such a program to train our people.

Professor Kayton concurred that quality patent searches were critical to the role of patent counsel and suggested that Landon IP organize a course under his guidance that could be taught to our employees and others. We accepted his offer and after extensive research and team effort, we produced a text for his programs. Several of our patent analysts and senior managers now teach at PRG. The text has been revised on several occasions and some of the content is included in this book. We also are happy to report that our patent search training courses at PRG are well attended and very successful.

We do not believe that our efforts have resulted in the definitive text on the topic. However, it remains our goal. We believe this book is a first big step, and we intend to revise it over time so that you, we, and others can benefit from a text that should have been written years ago.

Our goal is to provide you with approaches to patent searching that will be of benefit to you regardless of your technical expertise or role in the intellectual property community. Its focus is on principles and approaches and not on specific tools. Several database providers have effective search tools that we discuss in general. All of those companies will teach you how to use their software and services, and usually at no charge. Instead, this text is meant to teach you the art and science of patent searching regardless of the tools you use. We do offer criteria on how to select the appropriate search tools and even provide current information on the major databases.

We welcome any comments that you have on how we can continue to improve upon our efforts. Please contact me directly if you have any constructive advice to offer.

Thank you and best regards,
David Hunt, CEO
Landon IP, Inc.
dhunt@landon-ip.com
January 1, 2007
Alexandria, Virginia USA

CHAPTER 1

Patent Law and Examination as Context for Patent Searching

"If nature has made any one thing less susceptible than all others of exclusive property, it is the action of the thinking power called an idea, which an individual may exclusively possess as long as he keeps it to himself; but the moment it is divulged, it forces itself into the possession of every one, and the receiver cannot dispossess himself of it."

—Thomas Jefferson, Letter to Isaac McPherson, Monticello,
August 13, 1813

In hindsight, the third president of the United States and the driving force behind the establishment of America's first patent laws in 1790 was ahead of his time. Jefferson lived when a subject matter like biotechnology was known only vaguely; maybe through a farmer's knowledge of crop rotation, the use of manure, and the need for better soil preparation. Yet, the laws that he helped create still govern the practices of our present-day patent system and are able to encompass far-reaching technologies. Without knowing what the future held for intellectual property (IP), Jefferson crafted patent laws that continue to accommodate the review and prosecution of a myriad of technical subject matters.

During the early years of the U.S. Patent Office, a diligent search was important but not as difficult to carry out as it is now—considering a single cabinet ("shoe") held all of the patents ever granted. The burden of the

1

search was minimal on an inventor. In the present day, not only is a thorough search a "must" before entering patent prosecution (examination), but multiple searches at different stages in the life of a patent are now necessary. In the midst of our litigious culture, one has to be poised for unexpected miscues during their ideal patent term.

Patent searches before prosecution help improve the defensibility of the future patent, or can dissuade the inventor from prosecuting at all. Your preexamination preparation as an inventor, patent attorney, agent, or searcher will save the patent owner time and money later.

For example, consider spending US$25,000 to prosecute a patent application only to learn from the examiner that the invention lacks simple novelty. Worse, the examiner may not conduct an adequate search and you actually receive a patent that is later held invalid. The costs of that mishap will be enormous. A professional patent search will allow you to "look before you leap."

The many available search types that will be outlined in this text will yield invaluable data for an applicant who wants to increase their chances of earning a profitable return on a corporation's substantial investment.

The U.S. Patent System

Before discussing patent searching, it is first necessary to explain the patent system in the United States today, so that you and other readers can appreciate the challenges inherent in its navigation.

Thomas Jefferson's quote speaks to the uniqueness and idiosyncratic prospect of owning ideas, the building blocks of intellectual property (IP), and the challenges that exist in their maintenance and development.

Intellectual property consists of patents, trademarks, copyrights, and trade secrets. Article I, Section 8 of the United States Constitution empowers Congress to "promote the progress of science and useful arts by securing for limited times to authors and inventors the exclusive right to their respective writings and discoveries." Of the three types of intellectual property created by the Constitution, patents offer their inventors the strongest protection and, not surprisingly, present the highest hurdles to overcome in their application process.

To receive a patent, the inventor enters into a *quid pro quo* with the United States government or any other government where a patent is sought. In exchange for the exclusive right to manufacture, sell, and use his invention, the inventor provides to the public a full, enabling description of how to make and use the invention.

The Benefits of Patent Protection

Governments expect that with new, patented information in the public domain, more scientists will be encouraged to innovate with knowledge of these technological and scientific advancements. This fact may be counter-intuitive at first. You might argue that the public would actually benefit more if the inventor published their findings and shared their knowledge through the literary community. After all, the process would take less time and it is free. However, considering for example the patenting that occurs in biotechnology and the patenting of drug formulations, a company needs some assurance that they will have the exclusive right to a technology before they will invest millions in its development. Only a patent can give them this right.

In the United States, a pharmaceutical company has to invest heavily in initial research and development and subsequent testing and approval processes as required by the U.S. Food and Drug Administration (FDA).[1] This substantial investment provides reasonable assurance of a profit—in the form of patent protection—if research and development (R&D) is successful. The high cost of R&D also affects others, including the electronics, automotive, and energy industries. Patents grant them exclusive rights to the technology for limited times to recoup their costs and achieve profits.

A mere disclosure of technology in a publication may not spur commerce, as it does not guarantee any such right and only discloses the researcher's propriety information on which other groups may potentially build. Similarly, other inventions may require a great deal of groundwork or marketing before the invention included in their patent truly becomes accessible to and able to impact a field. In both of these scenarios, a large investment must be made by the patent owner (assignee) to prepare their invention to reach the public. Without having a guarantee for the exclusive right to manufacture, sell, and use a technology, it is highly unlikely that an entity would spend so much time, effort, and resources nurturing their inventions. A time period of exclusive control of patent rights affords the assignee the opportunity to recoup their research, development, or marketing costs inherent in the process.[2]

There are few assets that are as difficult to protect as IP. Therefore, it should not be a surprise that there are just as few assets in the global marketplace that demand the expertise of such a diverse population of professionals in order for the eventual worth of the technology to be realized. Patents have wide appeal across many fields, from a farmer in need of a genetically modified, insecticide-resistant soybean to a retired engineer who tinkers in his basement workshop, to a venture capitalist seeking a highly profitable investment opportunity—patents influence the choices of individuals in a variety of paradigms.

Readers may find themselves practicing their specialty in a variety of different fields: science, engineering, law, patent searching, or business development, to name a few. With the attention of such an educated and highly specialized group of professionals, obtaining and managing a patent throughout its life must not be an easy process; however, significant gains are expected once an exclusive right to a particular property is received.

The owner of a patent by right is its inventor; however, the inventor usually assigns his rights to his employer (corporation, university, or organization) in his employment contract. Therefore, the assignee has the exclusive right to the particular technology. The patent owner controls the ability to license the patented technology or to exclude others from making, using, or selling it.

Harmonization of Patent Laws

While a U.S. patent is enforceable only within the confines of the United States, there are steps being taken to harmonize the patent systems of the world, so one day many countries might have more uniform patent laws. A harmonized patent system will allow an inventor to receive patent protection in foreign countries more seamlessly. The goal of U.S. legislators is to protect an American patent holder's rights and to facilitate the filing and protection of patents internationally.

The Paris Convention   Much progress has been made to accommodate the prospect of such a system. The evolution began in 1885. The Paris Convention was first signed in that year and since has been adopted by every industrialized nation (except Taiwan). In addition to creating the concept of *priority*, which gives the patent holder up to 21 years of protection in most cases, the Convention afforded new freedoms to inventors of the adopting countries. An inventor from any of the signatory countries may file an application in any other member country within one year of the filing in their home country and receive the benefit of the home country's filing date during examination.

The Patent Cooperation Treaty Then, in 1970, the Patent Cooperation Treaty (PCT) was signed and adopted by 100 countries. This treaty allowed patent offices around the world to share in the burden involved in patent prosecution, such as the search and preliminary examination of an applicant's subject matter.

Trade-Related Intellectual Property Rights (TRIPS) More recently, the World Trade Organization's (WTO's) Trade-Related Intellectual Property Rights (TRIPS) agreement ushered in harmonization efforts, including patent agreements through the General Agreement on Tariffs and Trade (GATT) and North American Free Trade Agreement (NAFTA).

GATT was signed by U.S. President Bill Clinton in 1994 and introduced patent term alterations and the "provisional application" in America. Now U.S. patent filers may benefit from the same one-year increase in patent term as those applicants who had filed a foreign application in other countries. Before its implementation, the U.S. patent term was 17 years from the date of its issuance, subject to the payment of maintenance fees.

Following the agreement, the patent term was changed to 20 years from the date the application was *filed* in the United States, or 20 years from the earliest filed application if the application contains a specific reference to an earlier application filed under 35 U.S.C. 120, 121 or 365(c).[3] The 20 year patent term may also be extended by at most five years to compensate for various delays experienced during the patent's prosecution. The change to a 20-year patent term has also greatly reduced the occurrence of submarine patents in the United States.[4]

American Inventors Protection Act of 1999 (AIPA) Most recently, the United States passed the American Inventors Protection Act of 1999. The law requires that any application filed after November 29, 2000, be published and made publicly available after 18 months of filing an application with the USPTO,[5] except under special circumstances. Each of these acts has brought the U.S. system into closer alignment with the rest of the world.

The Priority Date

The concept of *priority* is fundamentally tied to patentability. The criticality of "filing dates" was mentioned earlier, and the "priority date" is defined by the earliest filing date. It is the date behind which the applicable reference (also known as "prior art") will be found. The priority date is crucial to several types of patent searches.

The U.S. Provisional Application   In order for inventors to enjoy the 21-year patent term in the United States, the provisional application was created after the GATT agreement. The inventor would submit the provisional application to the USPTO one year before his formal patent application and, if the patent is granted, obtains a year earlier priority and the possibility for a 21-year patent term. Thus, the provisional application is a placeholder in an applicant's chain of priority. It is never examined and it expires one year from its filing date.

Most importantly, the applicant's "priority date" is the earliest filed application (either in the United States or as a foreign application) that is recognized in the United States as a credible claim to priority (under 35 U.S.C. 120, 121, or 365(c)).

Continuing Applications   The continuing application can help preserve a priority date. In the United States, the continuation application, the divisional application, and the continuation-in-part may be filed, depending on your goals with regard to the examination process.[6]

Nonprovisional Applications   In the United States, you can file three types of nonprovisional patent applications: utility, design, and plant applications. Each has its own rules governing examination, but all are searched similarly.

Patent offices use a classification system to categorize patents into distinct technologies and to identify the particular claimed field in patent art.

Sometimes, a single invention may be described by multiple classification codes.[7]

The classification code also allows examiners and searchers to quickly narrow a search of the prior art to the particular subject matter of interest.

Sections of a Patent

The granted patent has many sections. At some point you will read each one of these sections to assist you in a search. The following table briefly describes the important sections of a U.S. patent. Many of these items also are printed on non-U.S. patents.

Section	Description
Front Page (The home of bibliographic data)	The front page of a U.S. patent or published patent application contains bibliographic data. This includes patent title, filing date, grant date, the name of each inventor, the patent owner (if disclosed during prosecution), priority data, and the filing dates and numbers of related patent applications. The front page includes the classes and subclasses assigned by the patent office to the document. It includes the list of classes and subclasses that the examiner searched during the prosecution process. Finally, it includes a list of all other patents and nonpatent literature cited by the applicant and the examiner as prior art during prosecution.
Abstract	The abstract provides a brief summary of the invention.
Specification	The specification is a lengthy written description of the underlying invention(s). It provides context for the invention and describes how a person of ordinary skill in the art can make and use the invention without undue burden.
Claims	The claims are most important. They define the scope of protection provided by the patent. The granted patent shows only the claims allowed by the examiner. The larger set of filed claims is accessible from the patent application and located in the official patent file history. In the United States, the claims must be interpreted in light of the specification.[8]
Drawings	The drawings provide details of the claimed invention.

(continues)

Section	Description
List of Cited References	Both the applicant and the examiner may cite patent and nonpatent references as prior art. The references cited by the examiner receive an asterisk (*) when printed on the granted patent. The most important references are those "considered" by the examiner and are not indicated on the patent. You would need to read the examiner's office actions located in the official patent file history to find the references that were considered by the examiner.

A Note about Reading the Specification and the Claims   Although the specification is lengthy, its content may serve only as a reference for defining the terms that are in the claims. Often, patent applicants attempt to argue limitations of their specification into their claims; however, "although the claims are interpreted in light of the specification, limitations from the specification are not read into the claims."[9] As a result, the wording of a claim and the way in which it is interpreted defines the scope of the invention and is the enforceable part of a patent. Therefore, skill, foresight, and information regarding the state of the art (obtained through a diligent search) should be relied upon by a patent professional before crafting the claims. As the searcher, you should carefully read and interpret the claims when determining whether to cite the patent during the search.

Sections of a Patent File History

Patent offices print only certain data from the examination on a granted patent. When required to conduct a thorough study of the patent, especially prior to a validity opinion, you should consult the official patent file history (see Exhibit 1.1).

The patent file history represents all the correspondence between the patent applicant and the examiner during prosecution. In addition to the material printed on the patent, the file history shows the claims as filed, the claims as prosecuted, arguments for and against patentability, appeals, petitions, references "considered" by the examiner, declarations, administrative papers, and documents specific to a technology (e.g., sequence listings for biotechnology applications). Our research indicates that up to 70 discrete

US006212461B1

(12) **United States Patent**   (10) **Patent No.:**   **US 6,212,461 B1**

Ghoneim et al.   (45) **Date of Patent:**   **Apr. 3, 2001**

(54) **EXTENDED BRAKE SWITCH SOFTWARE FOR VEHICLE STABILITY ENHANCEMENT SYSTEM**

(75) Inventors: **Youssef Ahmed Ghoneim**, Macomb Township, Macomb County; **David Michael Sidlosky**, Huntington Woods, both of MI (US)

(73) Assignees: **General Motors Corporation**, Detroit; **Delphi Technologies Inc.**, Troy, both of MI (US)

(*) Notice: Subject to any disclaimer, the term of this patent is extended or adjusted under 35 U.S.C. 154(b) by 0 days.

(21) Appl. No.: **09/322,041**

(22) Filed: **May 28, 1999**

(51) Int. Cl.^{7} **B60T 8/32**
(52) U.S. Cl. **701/70; 303/183; 303/191**
(58) Field of Search 701/70, 74, 76, 701/34; 303/122.04, 122.05, 177, 183, 191; 180/197

(56)   **References Cited**

U.S. PATENT DOCUMENTS

5,480,221	*	1/1996	Morita et al.	.... 303/113.5
5,720,533		2/1998	Pastor et al.	.... 303/147
5,746,486		5/1998	Paul et al.	.... 303/146

* cited by examiner

Primary Examiner—Michael J. Zanelli
(74) *Attorney, Agent, or Firm*—George A. Grove

(57)   **ABSTRACT**

A process is disclosed for use in a micro-processor managed brake control system that utilizes wheel speed sensors and a brake off/on switch when the system requires information as to whether the vehicle is experiencing hard braking. In accordance with the process, the average deceleration of the undriven wheels is estimated and the slip of each undriven wheel is estimated and the results are compared with pre-determined values for these parameters over a suitable test period. At the conclusion of these tests, the data may be used in place of data from a brake pedal position sensor or to confirm the data from such a sensor.

10 Claims, 2 Drawing Sheets

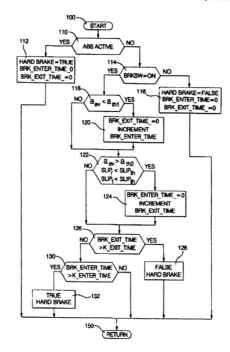

U.S. 6,212,461 B1

7

If BRK_Enter_Time has reached the pre-set value, K, the process proceeds to block 132 in which it is established that the hard brake situation is in effect. HARD BRAKE flag is turned on or set as TRUE indicating to controller 68 that the brake pedal travel sensor has been actuated in a hard braking situation. The process then proceeds to Return block 150 and awaits the next process Start cycle.

The HARD BRAKE flag, or its absence, is then utilized in a brake control process, or the like, such as those described above. Alternatively, the flag is used to confirm that the hard brake sensor is working properly and the process need not be repeated until it is determined that such a test should prudently be conducted again.

Thus, the process of this invention provides an initial test of hard braking once it has been determined that the ABS is not active and the break off/on switch is ON. The initial test is a comparison of the average deceleration of the undriven wheels with a predetermined threshold value of this parameter. If this test shows the possibility of hard braking then a break test timer is started. A more comprehensive group of undriven wheel acceleration and slip tests are than undertaken to better demonstrate the presence or absence of hard braking. Depending upon the results of this three part test the test enter counter is incremented or the test exit counter is incremented. No flag is set, no decision is made until the process has cycled a predetermined number of times and given a consistent answer.

While the invention has been described in terms of a preferred embodiment, it will be appreciated that other forms of the invention could readily be adapted by those skilled in the art. Accordingly, the scope of the invention is to be considered limited only by the following claims.

What is claimed is:

1. A method of determining a condition of hard braking in a vehicle having a brake off/on switch and a pair of undriven wheels, the method comprising:

   measuring the speed of each undriven wheel and determining the average deceleration of said wheels,

   determining wheel slip values of the undriven wheels and comparing said deceleration and slip values with predetermined threshold values of these parameters over a predetermined comparison period to determine a said hard braking condition.

2. A method as recited in claim 1 further comprising determining that the position of said off/on brake switch is on as a precondition to measuring said wheel speeds.

3. A method as recited in claim 1 further comprising determining that at least one of (a) the average deceleration of said undriven wheels and (b) a slip value of an undriven

8

wheel continually exceeds the respective threshold deceleration or wheel slip value over a predetermined comparison period before affirming a condition of hard braking.

4. A method as recited in claim 1 further comprising determining that the average deceleration of said undriven wheels and the slip values of both undriven wheels remain less than the corresponding deceleration and slip threshold values over a predetermined comparison period before affirming the absence of a condition of hard braking.

5. A method as recited in claim 1 further comprising using the result of the comparison of said deceleration and slip values in place of data from a brake pedal position sensor.

6. A method as recited in claim 1 further comprising using the result of the comparison of said deceleration and slip values to test data obtained from a brake pedal position sensor.

7. A method of determining a condition of hard braking in a vehicle having a brake off/on switch and a pair of undriven wheels, the method comprising:

   measuring the speed of each undriven wheel and determining the average deceleration of said wheels;

   making a first comparison test comprising comparing said average deceleration with a predetermined threshold value of said deceleration;

   determining wheel slip values of the undriven wheels; and

   making a second comparison test comprising comparing said deceleration and slip values with predetermined threshold values of these parameters;

   said measuring, determining and first and second comparison steps being repeated over a predetermined comparison test period to determine the presence or absence of a said hard braking condition.

8. A method as recited in claim 7 further comprising determining that at least one of (a) the average deceleration of said undriven wheels and (b) a slip value of an undriven wheel continually exceeds the respective threshold deceleration or wheel slip value over a predetermined comparison period before affirming a condition of hard braking.

9. A method as recited in claim 7 further comprising determining that the average deceleration of said undriven wheels and the slip values of both undriven wheels remain less than the corresponding deceleration and slip threshold values over a predetermined comparison period before affirming the absence of a condition of hard braking.

10. A method as recited in claim 7 further comprising using the result of said repeated comparisons in place of data from a brake pedal position sensor.

* * * * *

E X H I B I T   I . 2   **Example of Claims**

"papers" or entries can be found in a U.S. patent file history (see Exhibit 1.2).[10]

LOOK BEFORE YOU LEAP: CONSIDERATIONS BEFORE FILING

When Christopher Columbus sailed the ocean blue in 1492 he brought only the Niña, the Pinta, and the Santa Maria . . . not more than three ships and 120 men. *Why?*

For one, Columbus was unsure of what he would encounter in his attempt to find a sea passage to India. He and his sponsor, Spain, did not

want to invest all of their resources solely on the hope that he would succeed. The Spanish Monarchy was thrifty by commissioning a "search
party" to give them an idea of what to expect. At the outset, there was no
way of knowing how he would fare or what obstacles he would face.

After Columbus returned with his "search results," King Ferdinand and
Queen Isabella confidently sent more men on more expansive journeys, as
they now had understood the "lay of the land" and had fewer variables
about which to worry.

Now consider the hypothetical plight of a physician and his ill patient.
Upon learning of his illness, the doctor orders a diagnostic "search" of the
patient's entire body. He also conducts blood tests. His many searches are
intended to rule out possible causes of the patient's illness. When completed, the physician may have located a malignant tumor in the patient's
abdomen. He removes it and the patient lives another 20 years without a
reoccurrence.

These analogies illustrate the parallel between logical operators of every-
day life and those of patent prosecution. Why would you make a haphaz-
ard decision if you have the resources to reasonably predict or mitigate the
outcome?

Prior to filing a patent application of any kind, in the United States or
abroad, you should conduct one or more comprehensive patent searches.
If properly executed, the searches will suggest whether to file or not to file
the application, will assist with claims construction, and will help predict
the issues that will arise during examination.

Prior to prosecution, you should conduct a patentability search. With
sufficient time and budget, you also may wish to conduct a state-of-the-art
or a patent landscape prior to filing an application. The latter searches provide greater assurance that your efforts are not wasted.

This text describes all the major types of professional patent searches,
why they are conducted, when, and how. The discussion begins in Chapter 2.

PATENT EXAMINATION PROCESS

After conducting the appropriate search, patent applicants now have a better idea of what scope their claims should be and what to avoid claiming,
and hopefully will feel confident about their chances to eventually have
valuable patents in their portfolios.

The Job of the Patent Examiner

Broadly, patent examiners review patent applications for compliance with legal rules and procedures. Patent laws vary by country. In the United States, the U.S. Congress enacts patent laws, which are first interpreted by the USPTO and then by the federal courts when disputes arise.

The Examiner Follows the Courts   The U.S. Court of Appeals for the Federal Circuit (Federal Circuit) is often the final interpreter of major disputes; rarely will a patent case be heard by the U.S. Supreme Court. The Federal Circuit regularly interprets U.S. patent law and continually impacts the way in which patent applications are examined. The process is fluid and never stagnant.

The Examiner Follows Patent Examining Procedure   In the United States, patent examiners prosecute applications according the Manual of Patent Examining Procedure (MPEP). The USPTO publishes the MPEP to provide "patent examiners, applicants, attorneys, agents, and representatives of applicants with a reference work on the practices and procedures relative to the prosecution of patent applications before the Patent and Trademark Office."[11] In addition to practices and procedures, the MPEP contains references to U.S. laws and regulations.

Currently, the patent office requires practitioners to follow the fourth edition of the MPEP during prosecution. This is noted as a courtesy to new practitioners because often the USPTO admits individuals to the bar based on an examination of earlier editions. Until October 2006, for example, you needed to know the MPEP 2.0 to pass the patent bar, but you needed to know MPEP 4.0 to practice effectively.

Administrative Handling of the Patent Application   The patent process is lengthy, with pendency lasting several years after filing. In the United States, the applicant files the application by mail, hand delivery, or electronically (using EFS-Web). Upon receipt, the Office of Initial Patent Examination (OIPE) scans the document (if filed on paper), assigns an application number, reviews the document for "formalities," classifies the invention, and sends it to the appropriate Technology Center (formerly

Group Art Unit) for examination. After examination and allowability by the examiner, the case is transmitted to the Office of Publication (PUBS), which prints the granted patent. Specifically, PUBS prepares the case for printing, submits the file to a contract printer, publishes notice in the Official Gazette every Tuesday, and mails the patent grant to the applicant.

Actual Patent Examination   Actual patent examination includes several "rounds" of prosecution. With each round, patent examiners evaluate the most recently amended version of the claims and compare them to the vast body of patent and nonpatent literature. The examiner decides whether the process, machine, method, article of manufacture, or composition of matter being claimed is new, useful, and nonobvious to a person of ordinary skill in that subject matter.[12]

Sometimes, prosecution begins with a restriction requirement[13] limiting the inventor to the prosecution of a single invention. The applicant must elect the invention that will be prosecuted. The first substantive step is when the examiner issues a first action on the merits (FAOM) in the case. This first "office action" may provide the applicant with any number of rejections under 35 U.S.C. 101 *(utility)*, 102 *(novelty)*, 103 *(obviousness)*, and 112 paragraph 1 *(written description, new matter, and enablement)* and paragraph 2 *(indefiniteness)*.[14]

Each office action should lead the applicant closer to allowable subject matter by identifying the remaining issues or flaws in the inventor's application.

Based on our experience with the patent office, most examiners apply mainly art-based rejections and indefiniteness rejections under 35 U.S.C. 112, paragraph 2, in their office actions. This is true, for example, for patent applications that filed in Technology Center 1600 (Biotechnology). Examiners in 1600 regularly issue rejections under 35 U.S.C. 101 *utility*; and 112 paragraph 1, *written description and enablement*.[15] These rejections are made in addition to applying art from the patent and nonpatent literature located during the patentability search (see Exhibit 1.3). The specific steps in the U.S. examination process are illustrated in Exhibit 1.4.

Based on anecdotal statements by examiners, applying these statutes occupies roughly half of an examiner's time, and the search the other half. The examiner relies primarily on 35 U.S.C. 102 (a) (b) (e) and 103 (a) (obviousness) during prosecution.

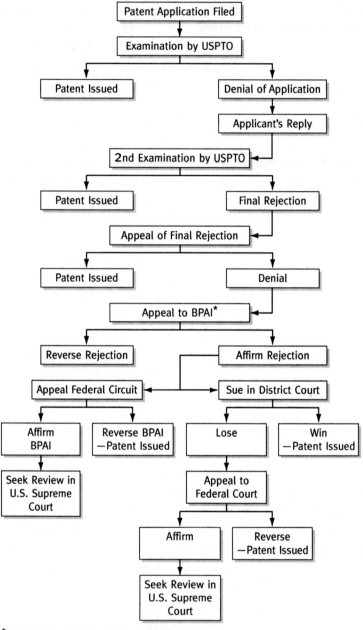

* Board of Patent Appeals and Interferences

E X H I B I T   I . 3   **Prosecution Flow Chart**

DETERMINE WHAT APPLICANT HAS INVENTED AND IS SEEKING TO PATENT
- Identify and Understand Any Utility and/or Practical Application Asserted for the Invention
- Review the Detailed Disclosure and Specific Embodiments of the Invention
- Review the Claims

↓

CONDUCT A THOROUGH SEARCH OF THE PRIOR ART

↓

DETERMINE WHETHER THE CLAIMED INVENTION COMPLIES WITH THE SUBJECT MATTER ELIGIBILITY REQUIREMENT OF 35 U.S.C. § 101
- Does the Claimed Invention Fall within an Enumerated Statutory Category?
- Does the Claimed Invention Fall within a 101 Judicial Exception — Law of Nature, Natural Phenomena, or Abstract Idea?
- Establish on the Record a Prima Facie Case

↓

EVALUATE APPLICATION FOR COMPLIANCE WITH 35 U.S.C. § 112

↓

DETERMINE WHETHER THE CLAIMED INVENTION COMPLIES WITH 35 U.S.C. § 102 AND § 103

↓

CLEARLY COMMUNICATE FINDINGS, CONCLUSIONS AND THEIR BASES
Review All the Proposed Rejections and Their Bases to Confirm Any Prima Facie Determination of Unpatentability.

EXHIBIT 1.4   Examination Process

The 102 (b) rejection is the strongest, as it represents a statutory bar. If a patent or nonpatent reference exists one year before the applicant's earliest filing date, the rejection under 102 (b) cannot be overcome by an inventor's declaration under 37 CFR § 1.131 or 1.132.

The Examiner Reviews Cited Patents and Nonpatent Publications
In the United States, patent applicants have a duty to disclose all known prior art references that would be of material interest to the examiner in their determination of patentability. This is accomplished with the submission of an Information Disclosure Statement (IDS) and Form 1449. In addition to his own search, the examiner reviews the patent and nonpatent literature filed with the IDS for its relevancy. Often, the filing of the IDS is the result of a patentability search by the applicant.

The Examiner Conducts an Inventor Search ("Double-Patenting" Search) Despite its importance, patent office approaches to searching vary greatly by the technology and an examiner's individual preferences and experience. There is no universal process, and most approaches are unstructured. However, the PTO requires examiners to conduct "inventor searches" to identify possible double patenting. Examiners conduct double-patenting searches of pending applications and granted patents.

Double-patenting rejections prohibit the improper extension of a patent term for a single invention. In other words, "the doctrine of double patenting seeks to prevent the unjustified extension of patent exclusivity beyond the term of a patent."[16]

The similarities in patent searching across examiners end with the double-patenting search. The following table shows some of the ways in which their approaches to searches may differ:

Type of Examiner	Usual *But Not Exclusive* Approach to the Search
Mechanical or Electrical	Focus heavily on the drawings and figures that are found in both patent and nonpatent literature.
Business Methods	Give special attention to Internet searches, as many business methods have applicability across fields.
Chemical	Focus heavily on both patent and nonpatent literature searches, but often conduct chemical structure and nucleic acid and protein sequence searches. They may send requests to the USPTO Scientific and Technical Information Center (STIC) where skilled searchers use proprietary databases[17] on their behalf.
Biotechnology	Review post–filing date art to find references that teach the unpredictability (the enablement of 112, paragraph 1) inherently present the biotechnology approach.[18] Further, these examiners rely on prior art for the provision of a "well-established" utility in a U.S.C. 101 sense.[19]

At some point the examiner has reviewed the references found through the patentability search, the double-patenting search, and the applicant's searches (as reflected on the Forms 1449). If it is an international application filed under the PCT, the examiner will also review the search report from the PCT (210) stage.

The Examiner Applies the References   The patent examiner will then apply the references against the intended claims of the applicant. He will apply the many patent law statutes and correspond with the applicant's attorney or agent through his written office actions.

Upon review of the examiner's office actions, the applicant may amend his claims in order to put them condition for allowance as prescribed by the examiner throughout the prosecution. He may also abandon the application in favor of continued prosecution, or he may appeal the examiner's opinion with the USPTO Board of Patent Appeals and Interferences (Board of Appeals).

If the Board of Appeals affirms the examiner's rejection, the applicant may appeal the decision to the U.S. Court of Appeals for the Federal Circuit (Federal Circuit). In practice, few applicants appeal either the examiner decision or that of the Board of Appeals.

Instead, the applicant abandons the case and either (1) prosecutes the subject matter in a continuing application or (2) amends the claims in order for the patent to be allowed. If unsatisfied with the protection provided by the granted patent, the applicant may file a continuation and attempt prosecution a second time.

Alternatively, the U.S. Congress has afforded the USPTO a limited role in reconsidering patentability decisions after patents are granted through reissue or reexamination proceedings.[20]

After Patent Grant

Maintenance fees are due on U.S. utility patents at 3.5, 7.5, and 11.5 years after patent grant. The PTO does not remind patent holders of this responsibility, but if unpaid, the patent will expire early.[21]

Also, following the granting of a patent, new possibilities present themselves to the owners of the patent in the form of licensing agreements. As a patent is property, it may be sold, mortgaged, or willed to another, just as any other form of property.

It is not necessary for a patent to be issued before it is licensed. Because of the high bar required for patentability, licensors often stipulate compensation even when a patent does not issue. Sometimes, this is a gamble for licensees. They may reap the first-to-market benefit of being the first to reveal the technology in a marketing effort.

BACKLOG OF PATENT APPLICATIONS

Several patent offices are faced with backlogs of unexamined applications, most notably the United States. Currently, the USPTO reports a backlog of 600,000 patent applications and is grappling with ways to expedite prosecution. The "average patent application pendency is 24.6 months"[22] and far from the PTO goal of 14 months.

In response, the PTO is continually hiring a record number of examiners and executing other measures to improve their situation. Among the other measures is hiring contractors to assist with the searching and examination of PCT searches (PCT/ISA 210 and 237). This began as a PCT Pilot Search program in October 2005. The USPTO later extended the pilot to longer-term contracts with qualified commercial search vendors.

We predict that the PTO will need to make more significant changes in the examination process to handle the backlog. There will continue to be a need for high-quality, professional patent searches in this process.

As more data is added to the public domain and the patent systems of the world become harmonized, the opportunities for profitable patent protection will increase.

NOTES

1. It can take years for a potential new drug to advance from an idea to a drug approved by the FDA, and can cost more than $800 million. (PhRMA. *Pharmaceutical Industry Profile* 2004.) There is only a 30 percent chance that an approved drug will produce revenues that match or exceed average research and development costs.
2. Of the patent system's twin purposes, encouraging new inventions and adding knowledge to the public domain, the economic justification is probably the most important rationale. (*The Disclosure Function of the Patent System (or Lack Thereof)*, 118 Harv. L.R. 2007, 2008 (2005)).
3. www.uspto.gov/web/offices/pac/doc/general/nature.htm.
4. "Submarine patent" is used to describe the practice of an applicant by which an originally unclaimed feature becomes a part of a claimed invention as a result of successively filed continuation applications. Literally, the patents undergoing this extended prosecution are submerged from the public within the PTO until the issuance of a patent. Prior to the passage of the AIPA in 1999, the United States did not publish applications until 18 months after filing, and therefore an inventor never had to publicly disclose their subject matter until their patent issued. As a result, a "submarined" patent would avoid being issued until more modern technologies had been incorporated into the application during its extended prosecution. In the end, the incorporation was somewhat anachronistic, considering that the novelty of many added claim limitations did not necessarily predate the application's filing date. As a result, considering the "secret" nature of the changes being made during its prosecution, many infringement suits naturally followed after its issuance. The GATT agreement shifted the financial consequences of a delayed prosecution onto the inventor, and

with the AIPA passage in 1999, 90 percent of all patents filed become published, according to a Federal Trade Commission report (How To Promote Innovation Trough Balancing Competition with Patent Law and Policy (2003); www.ftc.gov/opa/2003/10/cpreport.htm), limiting submarine patents. The most egregious prosecution of submarine patents was performed by the late Jerome H. Lemelson, who holds the top 13 places in American history of the longest patent prosecutions. Recently, many "Lemelson" patents have been ruled "unenforceable" due to the unreasonable and prejudicial delay taking place in their prosecution before the USPTO. (*Symbol*, 2004 WL 161331.)

5. Under 37 CFR 1.213, a nonpublication request can be made if the invention disclosed in an application has not been and will not be the subject of an application filed in another country, or under a multilateral international agreement that requires publication of applications 18 months after filing, the application will not be published under 35 U.S.C. 122(b) and § 1.211 provided:
   (1) A request (nonpublication request) is submitted with the application upon filing;
   (2) The request states in a conspicuous manner that the application is not to be published under 35 U.S.C. 122(b);
   (3) The request contains a certification that the invention disclosed in the application has not been and will not be the subject of an application filed in another country, or under a multilateral international agreement, that requires publication 18 months after filing; and
   (4) The request is signed in compliance with § 1.33(b).

6. See 35 U.S.C 119–121.

7. www.uspto.gov/web/patents/classification.

8. According to Fed. Cir. (CAFC) rulings as of 2006.

9. See *In re Van Geuns*, 988 F.2d 1181, 26 USPQ2d 1057 (Fed. Cir. 1993). The rampant practice of doing so can be seen in *C.R. Bard, Inc. v. United States Surgical Corp.*, where the court *imported the limitation* "pleated" into a broad claim reciting a surgical mesh plug used for hernia repair, relying heavily in doing so on the "Summary of the Invention" that described a plug having pleats. The court repeatedly referenced the Summary of the Invention throughout the opinion, notwithstanding the fact that 23 narrow claims of the 25 in the patent *did* recite a pleated plug, without even mentioning, let alone reconciling, the "immutable" doctrine of claim differentiation that should have sustained the broad claims." www.patentresources.com/advs06/adv_crfdrf.html.

10. This figure is based on a survey of U.S. patent file histories owned by Landon IP, Inc. as of 2006, numbering over 80,000.

11. www.uspto.gov/main/glossary/index.html.

12. A "useful" item is capable of achieving some identifiable benefit. *Juicy Whip, Inc. v. Orange Bang, Inc.*, 185 F. 3d 1364, 1366 (Fed. Cir. 1999). Novelty and nonobviousness are determined by comparing the invention with "prior art." *Graham v. John Deere Co. of Kan. City*, 383 U.S. 1, 15 (1966); 35 U.S.C.A. §§ 102(a)–(e), 103 (2005).

13. Under the statute 35 U.S.C. 121, the claims of an application may properly be required to be restricted to one of two or more claimed inventions only if they are able to support separate patents and they are either independent (MPEP § 802.01, § 806.06, and § 808.01) or distinct (MPEP § 806.05–§ 806.05(j)).

14. MPEP § 706.02–706.03(x).

15. Under the statute 35 U.S.C. 112, paragraph 1: "The specification shall contain a written description of the invention, and of the manner and process of making and using it, in such full, clear, concise, and exact terms as to enable any person skilled in the art to which it pertains, or with which it is most nearly connected, to make and use the same and shall set forth the best mode contemplated by the inventor of carrying out his invention." Written Description: "The claims contain subject matter which was not described in the specification in such a way as to reasonably convey to one skilled in the relevant art that the inventor(s), at the time the application was filed, had possession of the claimed invention." Enablement: "The claims contain subject matter which was not described in the specifica-

tion in such a way as to enable one skilled in the art to which it pertains, or with which it is most nearly connected, to make and/or use the invention."

16. "There are generally two types of double patenting rejections. One is the "same invention"–type double patenting rejection based on 35 U.S.C. 101, which states in the singular that an inventor "may obtain a patent." The second is the "nonstatutory-type" double patenting rejection based on a judicially created doctrine grounded in public policy and which is primarily intended to prevent prolongation of the patent term by prohibiting claims in a second patent not patentably distinguishing from claims in a first patent. Nonstatutory double patenting includes rejections based on either a one-way determination of obviousness or a two-way determination of obviousness. Nonstatutory double patenting could include a rejection that is not the usual "obviousness-type" double patenting rejection. This type of double patenting rejection is rare and is limited to the particular facts of the case. *In re Schneller*, 397 F.2d 350, 158 USPQ 210 (CCPA 1968)." www.uspto.gov/web/offices/pac/mpep/documents/0800_804.htm.

17. ABSS (Automated Biotechnology Sequence Search System) Coverage: Current, Full Text: Current Genetic sequence search system. USPTO internal genetic sequence search system composed of commercially available databases such as Genbank/EMBL, Geneseq, PIR, and UniProt. In-house databases (pending applications, issued patents, and published applications (PGPubs)) are also available for interference and prior art purposes. Useful for routine sequence searching as well as specialized searches, including alignments, length-limited, oligomer, and score/length.

18. For instance, if applicant is claiming "a method of diagnosing all types of cancers through the detection of a single nucleotide polymorphism (SNP) in the LSCP gene" and provides no corroborative data, an enablement rejection would be written and would cite the great unpredictability that exists in practicing such a method as portrayed in the post–filing date art. The best reference would teach that many studies have been done to show that SNPs in the LSCP gene are not reliably linked to all cancers.

19. An example of this scenario would be when a polynucleotide of a particular SEQ ID NO: with no specific or substantial utility asserted, has identity to a well-known or established family of biomolecules, the great identity affords it a "well-established utility" under 35 U.S.C. 101.

20. A post-grant review of patent claims under which third parties can request USPTO review takes place only under limited circumstances, including:
    - When a patentee files an application for reissue of a patent under 35 U.S.C. § 251 to correct at least one error in the patent,
    - When an applicant and a patentee claim the same invention and interference is declared pursuant to 35 U.S.C. § 135 between the patentee and the applicant, and the applicant seeks judgment based on the unpatentability of patent claims.
    - When a patent owner or third party requests the reexamination of a patent by means of either ex parte reexamination (35 U.S.C. § 302) or inter partes reexamination (35 U.S.C.§ 311). www.uspto.gov/web/offices/dcom/olia/reports/reexam_report.htm.

21. See 37, Code of Federal Regulations, § 1.366(c).

22. www.uspto.gov/main/faq/index.html.

CHAPTER 2

Types of Patent Searches

This chapter introduces the types of searches used by patent counsel to help assess patentability, validity, infringement, clearance, and state of the art. The text defines each search, suggests when the search is needed, and what types of art to review to ensure its completeness. The chapter does not discuss the mechanics of searching.

PATENTABILITY

What Is a Patentability Search?

Patentability searches (novelty searches) are conducted prior to the filing of a patent application. They help a patent attorney or agent determine whether an invention can be patented and, if so, what other patents or non-patent literature would be relevant to that assessment.

The patentability search seeks to determine if anyone disclosed the inventive concept in a publicly available work anywhere in the world before a date determined to be critical. The process includes a search of the prior art.

In order to receive a patent in the United States, the invention must be novel,[1] not obvious,[2] and have industrial applicability.[3]

Industrial applicability (or usefulness) is a prerequisite for a patent search. There is no reason, for example, to begin a search for an invention that is physically impossible, such as a machine for time travel.

Instead, the patent searcher focuses on the questions of novelty and obviousness. He finds written evidence that would dispute whether the invention is novel or would show that the invention would have been obvious to those skilled in the technological area. This means identifying duplicate inventions, if possible, and previously disclosed features of an invention by anyone.

When Is a Patentability Search Needed?   The patentability search is useful prior to preparing and filing a patent application. The results will help determine whether to pursue patent protection and may indicate what issues could arise during examination.

The search helps the writer of the patent application construct claims to achieve the broadest possible protection without treading on the known prior art. In others words, the searcher locates relevant patents and publications that inform the claims writer of the absolute limits of possible protection.

In the absence of claims before the drafting of an application for patent, the search results will be limited by the specificity of the end user's request. This becomes important during prosecution when claims interpretation will impact the applicant's intellectual property protection.

In the United States, patentability searches are not required for the filing of a patent application. Though we strongly recommend a patentability search before filing, we have learned at least two reasons why some fail to conduct them beforehand:

1. The inventor is so well versed in the technology through education, conferences, experimentation, and the reading of books and periodicals that he just knows the "state of the art." He can recognize that an invention is a significant advance without having to conduct the patent search.

2. The filer or owner of the patent application is hurried. The organization speculates that others are equally interested in obtaining patent protection on the same concept and need to file quickly. This is more of an issue in a "first-to-file" country compared to the United States, which is a "first-to-invent" country.

The first reason is short sighted, particularly when no one can be certain of who is inventing what, when, and where. The second reason is understandable. Nevertheless, we recommend conducting the patentability search sometime prior to or during examination to provide some assurance that you can really patent the inventive concept, to avoid potentially costly litigation later, and to assist you with the examination of claims during prosecution.

What Needs to Be Searched in a Patentability Search?   Because any relevant written evidence may impact novelty or obviousness, you should search full patent specifications and the claims and all available technical and nontechnical publications (e.g., product brochures and conference proceedings). Any written material that precedes the filing date of a patent application or the present, if the application has not been filed, should be included. What you search and how long you search is merely a function of your available time, your budget, and the public availability of the information.

In most countries, patent authorities assess novelty by whether an invention was patented or described in a printed publication anywhere in the world. Therefore, you should search the patents and published patent applications of all the major patent offices and any other countries where time permits.

Too often, patent applicants and their legal counsel limit their searches to selective sources (such as U.S. patents only), perhaps expecting the patent office to fill the void with its own search. This is a major mistake and one of reasons why some patents are easily invalidated or the subject of costly litigation.

Although patentability searches may end with the identification of duplicate inventions, other types of searches are by definition exhaustive; that is, they attempt to identify all art related to the scope of a disclosure. The exhaustive searches covered in the following sections include legal searches of patent validity, patent infringement, and state of the art.

What the Searcher Needs to Know to Search Successfully   The more the professional searcher understands the details of the invention and its points of novelty, the better the results he will achieve.[4] This fact cannot be overstated. Prior art that the searcher cannot locate may haunt the patent owner later. In fact, critical missed prior art may be used to invalidate the granted patent later.[5]

VALIDITY

What Is a Validity Search?

Validity searches (also called invalidity searches) are used to determine absolute novelty at the time of invention. For this reason, a validity search may be thought of as an exhaustive patentability search that has been conducted after publication of the patent application or issuance of the patent. With this search, the claims[6] are validated against all prior art.

When Is a Validity Search Needed?   The goal of a validity search is to locate evidence that the patent claims were granted erroneously due to either oversight or concealment of the prior art during the examination process. Validity searches often are the result of potential patent infringement or a potentially profitable business opportunity.

Examples:

1. **Invalidity.** An automotive company has been sued for patent infringement. In response, the company conducts a search to invalidate the patent of the accuser. By illustration, Fast Car Company has been selling a certain vehicle type with a certain type of spoiler. Sleek Car Company owns an unexpired patent claiming that very combination of vehicle type with spoiler. So, the legal counsel of Sleek Car informs Fast Car of the alleged infringement. Fast Car conducts an invalidity search and informs the accuser that the patent in question is invalid and, therefore, unenforceable. They cite art that discloses the subject matter of the Sleek patent before its filing. These are patent references that were not considered during patent prosecution of the Sleek patent.

2. **Enforcement readiness.** The owner of an infringed patent is considering a lawsuit. In preparation, the company conducts a search to validate its patent as a precursor to enforcement. Sleek Car Company owns the unexpired patent on the specific type of vehicle with that specific type of spoiler. They learn that Fast Car Company has been selling the same combination. Before incurring costly litigation, Sleek Car needs reasonable assurance of a successful outcome. The company also anticipates that Fast Car will defend itself by asserting the invalidity of the patent in question. Therefore, Sleek Car

conducts a validity search to assure the enforceability of the patent and to discover any previously unknown art that Fast Car may assert against the patent.

3. **Licensing.** The licensee conducts a validity search to ensure that proposed royalty payments are justified. The patent owner (licensor) also conducts a validity search, knowing that a highly defensible patent will command greater royalties. By illustration, Fast Car Company wants to sell the car with the spoiler combination, believing they are well positioned to reach the aftermarket. Meanwhile, Sleek Car Company owns the patent but does not manufacture or sell the vehicle/spoiler combination. Fast Car offers to pay Sleek Car royalties for the licensing rights to the patented invention. Before agreeing on the royalty amount, Fast Car Company conducts a validity search. Fast Car fears that another car manufacturer will quickly replicate the successful product; they want royalty payments if another competitor could freely replicate should the patent be invalid. Meanwhile, Sleek Car Company conducts its own validity search knowing that a highly defensible patent will command greater royalties.

Sometimes, upon issuance of your patent, another patent comes to your attention during an infringement search. It might appear that the claims of the other patent are broader than yours but fully encompass your invention. In an attempt to avoid potential litigation, you offer to in-license the other patented technology. Unfortunately, the company that owns the adverse patent is not interested in licensing to you.

You could decide to search to invalidate your competitor's patent. While this does not forbid a patent infringement suit, it provides some protection against the amount of damages awarded if a suit is filed. The process of establishing invalidity is not a trivial one. However, if you can prove that other patent is invalid, it could be shown that you did not willfully infringe on it.

What Needs to Be Searched in a Validity Search?   The subject features of the search are the claims (of a utility patent) or drawings (of a design patent). Patent and nonpatent literature is searched for relevancy prior to the earliest claimed priority date of the patent in question. In other words, you would analyze the same documentation as that of a patentability search except anything published after this critical date.

The search would include full patent specifications and claims of global patents filed on or before that date. It also would include any technical or nontechnical literature published on or before that critical date.

With a U.S. patent, the critical date is:

- The filing date of the U.S. patent or published application containing the claims to be validated.

- The publication date of a foreign or Patent Cooperation Treaty (PCT) equivalent of the U.S. patent or application if that publication date precedes the U.S. filing, and that filing claims foreign priority.

- The priority date established by the filing of a parent application that contains the claims to be validated, as can be the case when the patent at issue is a continuation or a continuation-in-part, for example.

Sometimes you will search art after the critical date. This might uncover references published slightly after the priority date, which actually may have been publicly available before the printed publication date. If you are a nonattorney searcher, agree on the critical date with the attorney who commissioned the search prior to start.

INFRINGEMENT

What Is an Infringement Search?

Infringement searches are used to determine whether an enforceable patent claims the same matter as your concept or unpatented invention. Accordingly, the document set for these searches consists of only unexpired (in-force) patents.

Ideally, you would begin the search by comparing a set of written claims against the claims of relevant in-force patents. Without written claims, you could proceed with a written description from which you could draft a set of hypothetical claims. Patent claims that read on the subject matter of the disclosure can be said to read on the real or hypothetical claims to which the search is directed.

Although a patent offers an exclusive right to the patent holder, it does not expressly provide the right to practice the invention in an environment where another issued patent broadly encompasses the claimed subject matter.

Broadly, the infringement search:

- Provides the applicant with the existence of issued U.S. patents (if their filing will be in the United States) that claim the same subject matter as that which they intend to include in their filing.
- Includes a search of all enforceable (normally at least 20 years earlier than applicant's filing date) claims of U.S. patents and published applications.
- Compares applicant's proposed claims (most often independent) to those issued or pending.
- Compares applicant's claims to a broader claim that is encompassing of applicant's invention found in the issued patents.

A useful tool in your analysis is a claims comparison chart that compares the in-force patent claims with the subject matter of the disclosure. Such a tool is presented in Chapter 5.

When Is an Infringement Search Needed?   The patent infringement search is needed prior to making, using, or selling a product or service where you might suspect the evidence of patented technology. Because of its heavy focus on claims, it is sometimes conducted prior to drafting claims in your own patent applications.

In the United States, which is a "first-to-invent" country, some companies will monitor their competitors closely, read the claims of every published patent application their competitor has filed, copy the claims verbatim in their own filing, and file a resulting patent application. This is done when you are certain that you were first to invent the concept and reduce it to practice. It is a very effective approach to initiating an interference with another filer when you are certain of your case.

What Needs to Be Searched in an Infringement Search?   A professional infringement search is directed to the claims of all in-force patents and patent applications. You would search the patent documents of the country or patent authority of alleged infringement. Unless otherwise directed, you would not search expired patents or patents that expired for failure to pay maintenance fees. You would not search the patent documents of countries or authorities where infringement has not been alleged. You would not search nonpatent literature.

You should seek to locate not only the exact claimed invention, but one of broader scope. For example, if the newly issued patent claim was drawn to a method of making cappuccino, and the infringement search revealed a method of making coffee in an earlier issued patent, a possible infringement may occur.[7,8]

Many patent attorneys appreciate any additional information that assists with their assessment of infringement. For example, the current legal status of any relevant patent can impact the direction of an infringement opinion. A professional patent searcher will often provide supplemental information about relevant patents, such as patent adjustments and extensions.

In recent years, a larger percentage of U.S. patents have been found valid and infringed. This is an interesting fact that has been the result of legislation, the establishment of the U.S. Court of Appeals for the Federal Circuit (CAFC), and the direction of U.S. case law.

CLEARANCE

What Is a Clearance Search?

Clearance searches ("right-to-use" or "freedom-to-operate" searches) are used to determine whether a party has "clearance" to make, use, and sell an inventive concept. Clearance is established when a patent has not been infringed or has otherwise expired.

When Is a Clearance Search Needed?   The clearance search is needed prior to bringing a product to market. The organization wants to avoid alleged infringement when making, using, or selling a product or process. Moreover, the organization seeks the added assurance, if possible, that the business decision will be supported by patents or published information in the public domain.

The clearance search usually accompanies a clearance opinion drafted by patent counsel that forecasts the potential for infringement of an issued patent's claims or those of a pending patent application.

Because claims define the invention, claims endure scrutiny throughout the life of the patent. They should fully reflect the inventor's understanding of the scope of the technology when they are drafted.

The clearance search is broader than an infringement search because you also seek to determine where the technology may be used or protected around the world (not just in the country of possible infringement), and whether it may be used freely without allegations of infringement or the need for licensing.

Patents are only enforceable in the country or governmental region in which they were granted. You may have the patent in the United States and not China, for example. You later recognize that your protected innovation in the United States is widely practiced in that country.

The clearance search may reveal, through nonpatent literature, who else has been practicing your invention. You also may reveal the existence of multiple patenting; a patent in one country and a patent in the other. In this event, one of the patents might be invalid because the existence of the other patent was not cited as prior art during a patentability search.

The search may establish where a potentially unexploited market exists; and therefore, where the patent owner or applicant could manufacture, use, sell, or license the invention.

The search also could be conducted after receiving your granted patent. Especially since the prosecution could take years and the state of the art is inevitably going to have changed in that time period. When you consider that many patent applications are subject to publication after 18 months from the priority filing (an application may still be in prosecution at this point), it is very important that a patent holder survey what the public has done with the disclosure of that technology. The sooner the patent holder knows about potential competition in the United States or abroad, the sooner they can begin the work to challenge it and defend their property.

What Needs to Be Searched in a Clearance Search?   You can think of clearance searches as a combination of patentability and infringement in terms of the breadth of patent and nonpatent literature that needs to reviewed, as well as attention that you should give to enforceable patent claims. Unless otherwise directed, the professional clearance search includes a review of global patents and published patent applications, both expired and unexpired, and all available nonpatent literature. The objective is to learn what exists in the public domain and, therefore, is free to use.

The subject matter may be the actual or hypothetical claims. As opposed to infringement, however, you should carefully consider the application of the subject matter.

STATE OF THE ART

What Is a State-of-the-Art Search?

The state-of-the-art search is a comprehensive search of all available patent and nonpatent literature. The searcher does not focus on a single invention, but assembles all references that relate to a defined technical field. When assembled, the technical references should reflect the current "state of the art." The search usually results in a large set of references.

The breadth and depth of the search depend on how closely the technology was defined at the start. If you define the technical scope as "liquid crystal display" instead of "active matrix liquid crystal display," you will read many more patents and spend more time on the project.

We have found it useful to narrow or broaden the scope during the search in order be comprehensive but productive. It is an iterative process even when you have a precise understanding of the technology you intend to search.

When Is a State-of-the-Art Search Needed?   Some scientists and product development teams conduct state-of-the-art searches to determine the direction of research activities. Business development teams conduct them prior to the marketing of a technology or to assist them with licensing. Some companies conduct them to reassess the importance of their patent portfolio and technical contributions to a joint venture. Sometimes they help indicate the opportunity for a strategic business acquisition.

Many patent attorneys use them to assist with a patentability opinion, believing that a broad state-of-the-art search is more useful to them than a targeted novelty search. The search that you conduct or commission should depend on the business or legal requirements you are trying to address.

What Needs to Be Searched in a State-of-the-Art Search?   State-of-the-art usually includes a search of global patents and published patent applications, and nonpatent literature. It is not limited to unexpired patents, like an infringement search. Nevertheless, every search is customized and depends on the objectives that have been established by the search recipient.

If you know of a significant event, such as the patent that created an industry, you might begin your search there. For example, it is not necessary to search recombinant DNA (gene splicing) prior to the filing of the Cohen/Boyer patent, U.S. 4,237,224. In this case, your search might begin in 1980.

While the search focuses on the current state of the art, the same technology assessed over a longer time period is often referred to as a "collection search."

PATENT LANDSCAPE

What Is a Patent Landscape Search?

One very comprehensive state-of-the-art search is a patent landscape study. The patent landscape search is a deeper analysis of patent and nonpatent references after completion of the state of the art. The study often results in the categorization of patents into fundamental discoveries versus incremental improvements, a visual display of patenting over time periods, the history of a technology's development, and even analyses of inventor collaborations. The patent landscape study may further identify key innovative groups over defined periods of time.

It is often conducted to determine whether to enter a specific research area. A landscape can significantly improve your ability to make business decisions by providing an overview of patent activity in specific technology areas. Using aspects of competitive intelligence, a landscape study is something that could anticipate any product liability issues in the future. The patent landscape study helps:

- Monitor markets of interest
- Identify gaps in and improve your research and development
- Determine which of your prospective patents will have significant commercial value
- Confirm which inventions are now in the public domain
- Better understand current competitors and identify future ones

BENEFITS OF PRIOR ART SEARCHING

In summary, there are several benefits to conducting patent searches of the types we discussed. The search you conduct or commission will be a reflection of your objectives. When done, you should have a better sense of your business and legal options. Nevertheless, the search itself does not replace a fully informed legal opinion that must be provided by capable legal counsel.

Your positions or options may be:

- Proceed confidently as initially thought, since no prior art was found and no issued claims loom as infringement hazards.

- Crisis averted—Potential infringers were found and require that an applicant reevaluate his or her intentions for prosecution. It could be possible to prosecute another part of the inventor's research instead, now that you have seen its potential in the search results.

- Don't go it alone—A thorough freedom to operate or prior art search revealed inventors/corporations who may be approached for prefiling licensing and collaborating in future product development and marketing.

- Better now than later—Prior art was found in the novelty search, but the claims can be amended to obviate a rejection made using the reference. The art will also be submitted to the patent office so that it can be made of record in the case and eventually printed on the face of the patent.

- Untapped resources after all—The landscape study revealed that some of the patents the applicant already owns in his or her portfolio may prove to be more lucrative if licensed to particular companies rather than patenting the originally intended invention.

- Two wallets are better than one—A small company was able to find possible licensees for the marketing of their product.

- Do not reinvent the wheel—A couple of inventors are especially successful in areas of research that interests you; it is now possible to reach out to them for collaboration.

NOTES

1. For *novelty*, the invention must be demonstrably different from publicly available ideas, inventions, or products (so-called "prior art"). This does not mean that every aspect of an invention must be novel. New uses of known processes, machines, compositions of matter, and materials are patentable. Incremental improvements on known processes may be patentable.
2. For *obviousness*, the invention cannot be obvious to a person of "ordinary skill" in the field; nonobviousness usually is demonstrated by showing that practicing the invention yields surprising, unexpected results.

3. For *usefulness*, the invention must have some application or utility or be an improvement over existing products and/or techniques.

4. Taking as an example a scenario from a nucleic acid search in biotechnology: The patent information scientist was given a broad request: "Could you please search the *BRCA1* gene?" (Breast Cancer 1: very well known gene that encodes a nuclear phosphoprotein that plays a role in maintaining genomic stability and acts as a tumor suppressor). The absence of an enumerated sequence or reference to an accession number makes the search incredibly broad. A cursory search revealed 3,867 different records (each with multiple revision histories) of the *BRCA1* gene. Furthermore, it is not clear what the scope of applicant's invention is. Is the search to "comprise" the sequence (i.e., have the sequence and have anything else on either side of the sequence?) or is their request for the sequence that just "consists of" *BRCA1*? Depending on what the inventor is eventually claiming—"the sequence comprising *BRCA1*," "the sequence consisting of *BRCA1*," "a nucleotide sequence of *BRCA1*," "a nucleic acid represented in *BRCA1*," "a complement of *BRCA1*," "a nucleotide sequence consisting of SEQ ID NO:X," etc.—the search will be entirely different. While examination and claim interpretation is outside of the purview of this book on searching, it should be noted that the subsequent use of the above "opened or closed language" in an applicant's claim set will alter the patentability of the invention and make the requested search less applicable. Always communicate the real inventive concept to the searcher.

5. Unpublished Foreign Patent Application Invalidates Later Filed Patent: *Bruckelmyer v. Ground Heaters* (Fed. Cir. 2006). http://patentlaw.typepad.com/patent/2006/04/unpublished_ for.html. Posted by: Dennis Crouch, April 21, 2006. This case discussed the ruling that figures from a Canadian application file were deemed both "publicly accessible" as printed publications as the file was publicly accessible through a search of the Canadian Intellectual Property Office Web site public search page.

6. Usually one or more of the independent claims.

7. A patent holder can bring an infringement action against persons who make, use, or sell the patented invention; those who actively induce patent infringement; and those whose acts constitute contributory infringement. 35 U.S.C.A. § 271 (2005).

8. Where less than $1 million is at risk, the cost of litigation through appeal can reach $500,000; where $1 to $25 million is at risk, that figure rises to $2 million, and where more than $25 million is at risk, average costs are as high as $3,995,000. (Miller J. Building a Better Bounty: Litigation—Stage Rewards for Defeating Patents. 19 Berkeley Tech. L. J. 667 (2004).)

CHAPTER 3

The Mechanics of Searching

This chapter teaches an effective approach for scoping a search. It describes the different types of patent searches; proposes criteria and methods for determining the relevancy of patent references; discusses the importance of certain sections of the patent for determining relevancy; and presents the benefits of classification, full text, and citation searching. The chapter also presents issues that are peculiar to different types of subject matter and how to address them.

INTRODUCTION

Before digitized patent information was available, a patent search consisted of a manual review of paper patent documents directed only by available classification and indexing systems. In the United States, a patent search involved literally flipping through patents stored in "the shoes" or filing cabinets of the U.S. Patent and Trademark Office (USPTO). The way to navigate patents was by relying exclusively on the patent classification system to guide you. Patents that were misclassified were usually missed. The original patent search, in its purest form, was a patent classification search.

Since the arrival of digitized patent information, the text search has become an integral part of—and for some practitioners, the only approach to—patent searching. Because it is possible to text search across all available patent classification areas simultaneously, some searchers rely on text searching exclusively with the notion that such a search is more targeted and "outlier" misclassified patents will be captured that otherwise would not be included in a strict classification search. Broadly speaking, a text search is any query where free text is entered to retrieve results.

Text searching can encompass a search across any patent data field and not just matching text phrases in the body of a patent. Text searching can include an inventor search, a search for a specific filing date, an assignee (owner) search, or many others.

In addition to text queries, searchable patent information has made citation searching very easy. As this chapter will discuss, citation searching is a review of the documents *cited by* a patent of interest, as well as a review of the documents *citing* the patent of interest.

As patenting activity has continued to increase at a staggering rate, so has available patent information. The sheer volume of patent information currently available is a reflection not only of fundamental technological advancements, but an increasingly wider variety of improvements that are made to each new fundamental discovery. In short, the number of variations of each invention is increasing.

Consequently, it is more difficult than ever to be a true subject matter expert simply due to the pace and breadth of innovation. The volume of patent information renders a straightforward and linear patent search ineffective.

Before beginning a search you should consider the following concepts at all times:

- A patent search is a learning process in and of itself.
- A patent search is continually iterative.

The searcher or information scientist will learn, for example, alternate embodiments of the invention in hand through the course of the search, and the searcher must use this knowledge to continually refine his or her search methodology.

It is crucial in any search for prior art that *all three* basic search mechanisms be used appropriately—that is, classification searching, text searching, and citation searching.

One exception to this guideline is applied when searching very new technology where classification schedules may lag behind the technology. When this happens, the corresponding classification schedules do not have as many subcategories (or subclasses) as they should. We discuss this point further in the section on biotechnology searches.

The search steps discussed in this chapter illustrate a systematic way of searching patent documents. A large proportion of the chapter, however, is dedicated to preparing for the search. This includes properly scoping the subject matter, properly scoping the classification areas to be searched, and properly generating initial text queries. All of these steps are important to achieving a systematic and methodical search.

Please note that when discussing steps that require evaluating the results of a search query, either during search scoping or in conducting the search, this text assumes that the searcher is familiar with and is using an electronic search engine.

By definition an *invention* is a discovery or finding.[1] However, many practitioners in the patent community consider an invention only a discovery or finding that has been deemed useful, novel, and nonobvious. For clarity, the term *invention* is used in this chapter to describe an idea that is provided to the searcher for the purposes of a patent search. This may come in the form of a simple, informal disclosure, a fully drafted patent application, or an issued patent, depending on the type of search requested (see Chapter 2).

PROPERLY SCOPING THE SEARCH

Identifying Subject Features: Problem-Solution Approach

Necessity is the mother of invention. Inherently, all inventions fill a need by solving a problem. The solution to the problem includes what the invention *is* and what the invention *does*. This is an important distinction to make prior to embarking on the search.

As you scope the search, your first step should be to compartmentalize the invention into discrete, searchable features by answering these questions:

- What problem does the invention solve?
- What is the invention?
- What does the invention do?

If this seems overly simplistic, you will see the importance of answering these questions thoroughly and literally in the exercises that follow.

We will illustrate this approach using a sample invention. This example will help communicate several concepts in the chapter. Let us begin with a high-speed car chase:

> *High speed police chases are a danger to people and property. The amount of time a high-speed chase continues will increase the chances of civilian or material harm. To prevent these chases from occurring, the need has arisen for a remote car disabling mechanism used by police officers to impede the progress of the getaway car. The mechanism would incorporate a tamper-proof receiver installed by default in every automobile upon manufacture that responds to the signal from a transmitter to cut the fuel supply and ignition to the engine. The receiver is connected to a relay that may cut off power to a vehicle's electric fuel pump or activate a cutoff valve. The relay also cuts power to the ignition pack or distributor. Transmitters and control modules are installed in all police vehicles. The officer may use the control module to select the vehicle that requires disablement by identification (e.g., license plate number) and transmit a fuel-cutoff signal to the appropriate vehicle. The officer may be in a police vehicle such as a patrol car or helicopter.*

See the following table for the answers to the key questions for the preceding example.

What problem does the invention solve?	High-speed **police chases** are a danger to people and property.
What is the invention?	A **control module**, a **transmitter**, a **receiver**, optionally a **valve**, and at least one **switch**.
What does the invention do?	**Remotely disables** a **car** in motion by **cutting off** the **fuel** supply and **ignition**.

When answering these questions, you will see important keywords emerge as shown in bold in the preceding table.

It would be easy to answer the question "What is the invention?" with a response like "A device that remotely disables a car by cutting off the fuel supply and ignition." However, this does not describe what the invention physically is. If you had to set the invention on the table in front of you, what would you see?

You would likely see the hardware components that make up the device itself—the control module, transmitter, receiver, valve, and switch. Looking at these items on a table, you might not have any idea how they work together. (This illustrates the importance of answering these questions very literally.)

When the invention is a method, it is even more important to very carefully make the distinction between what the invention is and what it does. Consider the following example:

The invention is a method for a law enforcement officer to stop a high-speed police chase by first selecting the vehicle to be disabled from the pursuing police vehicle, sending a disabling signal to the getaway vehicle, and cutting off the fuel supply and ignition to the getaway vehicle.

See the following table for the answers to the preceding key questions.

What problem does the invention solve?	High-speed police chases are a danger to people and property.
What is the invention?	A method having the steps: 1. Selecting the getaway vehicle 2. Sending a disabling signal to the getaway vehicle 3. Cutting off the fuel supply and ignition to the getaway vehicle
What does the invention do?	Remotely disables a car in motion by cutting off the fuel supply and ignition

Generating Keywords Returning to our original example, the invention is itself a solution. The solution includes what the invention actually is and what the invention does. These will be referred to as the invention's "structure" and "function" respectively. Therefore, the preceding key questions can be expanded to create the following invention diagram template:

Problem		High-speed police chases are a danger to people and property.
Solution	What it is: (structure)	Control Module Transmitter Receiver Valve Switch
	What it does: (function)	Remotely disables a car in motion by cutting off the fuel supply and ignition

This simple tool serves as a template to brainstorm initial keywords and terms. These are not actual search queries but terms that can be used to assemble search queries. It is a way to be exhaustive in capturing all terms that could be associated with the invention.

The terms include *synonyms* and *equivalents* that can be associated with each part of the invention. It forces you to address each part of the invention in a methodical way. Equivalents are different from synonyms in that they are alternate parts or steps that will make the invention work the same way and serve the same purpose. They can be thought of as alternate embodiments of the invention. For example, if the invention is a handheld instrument that deposits a substance onto a surface for the purpose of writing, the substance could be ink, graphite, charcoal, wax, or many others. Since the invention is for writing, glue may not be an appropriate equivalent to include, even though handheld instruments that contain glue are very common. A completed invention diagram of likely equivalents and synonyms for the sample invention follows.

Problem			Police, Law Enforcement Chase, Pursuit, Pursue
Solution	What it is: (structure)	Control Module	Control, Module, Terminal, Computer, Station Identify, Locate, Determine, Match, Choose, Select, Find Screen, Display, Keypad, Touchpad, Interface Chase Vehicle, Pursuing Vehicle, Police, Law Enforcement
		Transmitter	Radio, Infrared, Ultrasonic, Wi-Fi, Bluetooth, Satellite, Laser Transmit, Send, Signal, Message, Data Pursuing Vehicle, Chase Vehicle, Police, Law Enforcement
		Receiver	Radio, Infrared, Ultrasonic, Wi-Fi, Bluetooth, Satellite, Laser Receive, Reception, Signal, Message, Data Getaway Vehicle, Pursued Vehicle
		Valve	Valve, Restrictor
		Switch	Switch, Relay
	What it does: (function)		Remote, Range, Distance Disable, Impede, Block, Prevent, Inhibit, Restrict Vehicle, Car, Truck, Van, Automobile Cut off, Shut off, Turn off, Disconnect, Break

Fuel pump, Fuel line, Fuel injection,
Fuel injector
Ignition, Distributor, Spark, Plug, Wire,
Battery, Power, Electric

It is important to note how much more information was gathered by brainstorming when compared to the cursory information contained in the original invention description. This also illustrates how risky it can be to jump into the search without carefully dissecting the invention beforehand. We will return to the invention diagram to generate text search queries later in this chapter.

Selecting Classification Areas

As stated earlier, the earliest form of a patent search consisted of a search through classification areas. Since patent classification systems were designed to assist with patent searching, they are a good place to start.

We begin with the U.S. classification system because USPTO patent examiners will assist the public (except during an invalidity search) in navigating and selecting among cryptic class and subclass descriptions. Secondly, it is easy to identify corresponding international patent classification (IPC) codes by way of a concordance once the U.S. classification areas for the search are known.

U.S. Patent Classification (USPC) System   The USPTO uses several methods to classify patents, including:

- Industry or use (e.g., "metal foundry")
- Proximate function (e.g., "dispensing") (fundamental, direct, or necessary)
- Effect or product (e.g., the product of a manufacturing process or a system that produces an effect repetitively, such as "cookie-cutting machine" or "telephone system")
- Structure (e.g., a chemical structure or a metal alloy)

The organization of each patent class is framed around one or more of these rationales. You will discover that the U.S. classification schedule is not consistent in this regard. For example, in Class 5—Beds—subclass 635,

". . . combined with a table" is structural in nature, where subclass 637, ". . . adapted to immobilize head or neck" is functional. Subclass 635 is structural because patents in this subclass have a table physically attached. Patents in subclass 637 perform the *function* of immobilizing the head or neck using *any* structural device.

Because of similar discrepancies throughout the U.S. classification schedule, in addition to sometimes cryptic subclass titles, you can use four different methods to find the appropriate classification areas for a search:

1. Using the United States Patent Classification (USPC) Index
2. Searching keywords in the Manual of Classification
3. Reviewing a small set of closely related patents for their classifications
4. Consulting a USPTO patent examiner

The first two methods are provided on the USPTO Web site (www .uspto.gov). They are briefly discussed here but are left for you to explore further.

USPC Index (www.uspto.gov/web/patents/classification/uspcindex/ indextouspc.htm)   Using the earlier invention description, which primarily pertains to motor vehicles, we can begin to find classification areas by clicking on "V" to look up "Vehicle." Viewing the hierarchy under "Vehicle," we notice that motor vehicles are classified generally in class 180. In an attempt to be as specific as possible, we find a category called "Safety Promoting Means . . . 180/271+," which refers to Class 180, Subclass 271+. Clicking on "271+" brings us directly to the Manual of Classification for subclass 271. Looking down the list of subclasses within 271, we will see subclass 287 "By preventing unauthorized or unintended use or access." This is a great subclass to start reviewing patents once we have collected a comprehensive list of classification areas.

USPC Keyword Search (www.uspto.gov/web/patents/classification/) By searching for "motor vehicle" in the search field on the right side of the page, you will notice that the third result returned is "Class Definition for Class 180—Motor Vehicles." Clicking on this result displays the definition of the class as well as the subclasses. This method is more cumbersome and involves reviewing many subclass definitions.

Reviewing Closely Related Patents   Many experienced patent searchers start a classification search with this approach. This method assumes that you are familiar with the basics of a patent search engine.

Keyword search across the U.S. patent database for a small number of very closely related patents. Search narrowly within the TITLE and ABSTRACT. Seek out the most recently published granted patents possible since the classification schedules are reorganized every few years. Ignore published applications in this step because applications may be classified differently by the examiner just before issue.

Look up class titles/descriptions for the classes listed in the "U.S. Cl." section on the patents' first pages to determine the relevancy of these classes.

Look up class titles/descriptions for the classes listed in the "Field of Search" to identify any peripheral classes.

Using our example, a narrow search within the title and abstract fields across all issued U.S. patents yields several possibly relevant patents:

- U.S. 6,411,217—Issued 6/25/2002—Vehicle disabling system
- U.S. 6,135,226—Issued 10/24/2001—Means for selectively disabling a vehicle
- U.S. 6,072,248—Issued 6/6/2000—Method for externally and remotely disabling stolen or unauthorized operated vehicles by pursuing police and the like
- U.S. 5,861,779—Issued 1/19/1999—Car theft and high-speed chase prevention device
- U.S. 5,611,408—Issued 3/18/1997—Vehicle disabling device

By reviewing the first patent, U.S. 6,072,248 (the '248 patent), the three classification areas in the "U.S. Cl." field on the face of the patent prove to appear relevant.

U.S. Subclass 307/10.2

ELECTRICAL TRANSMISSION OR INTERCONNECTION SYSTEMS

VEHICLE MOUNTED SYSTEMS

Automobile

Antitheft

U.S. Subclass180/287

MOTOR VEHICLES

WITH MEANS FOR PROMOTING SAFETY OF VEHICLE, ITS OCCUPANT OR LOAD, OR AN EXTERNAL OBJECT

By preventing unauthorized or unintended access or use

U.S. Subclass 340/825.72

COMMUNICATIONS: ELECTRICAL

SELECTIVE

Frequency responsive actuation

Wireless link

Reviewing several of the classification areas in the "Field of Search" category on the face of the patent reveals that at least one no longer exists. Subclass 340/426 is extinct. Upon reviewing the schedule for class 340, it becomes apparent that subclass 426 was divided into 426.1 through 426.36. Upon review of subclass 426.1, it seems likely that it corresponds to the previous subclass 426 and includes land vehicle alarms or indicators "of burglary or unauthorized use."

After reviewing several patents in the list and repeating the process described earlier, we can arrive at a comprehensive list of classification areas with which to start.

Class 340: ELECTRICAL COMMUNICATIONS

Subclasses: 825.69, 825.72, 902, 904, 426.1, 426.11, 426.13, 426.16, 426.17, 5.2

Class 180: MOTOR VEHICLES

Subclasses: 287, 283, 284

Class 307: ELECTRICAL TRANSMISSION OR INTERCONNECTION SYSTEMS

Subclasses: 9.1, 10.2

Class 123: INTERNAL COMBUSTION ENGINES

Subclasses: 332, 333, 334, 335

Class 342: COMMUNICATIONS: DIRECTIVE RADIO WAVE SYSTEMS AND DEVICES

Subclass: 44

Frequently, even closely related patents will contain classification areas that are not related. These patents are ones that discuss specific features that are not important to the invention in hand for the search. For example, one of the areas uncovered in the preceding cursory search is subclass 341/176:

CODED DATA GENERATION OR CONVERSION

Code Generator or Transmitter

Transmitter for remote control signal

Since the sample invention disclosure does not discuss coding of the activation signal, Class 341 is outside the scope of the invention disclosure and is an area that is appropriate to exclude from the search.

Finding Subclasses with the Help of a Patent Examiner It is not widely known that U.S. patent examiners are available to the public for the purpose of providing assistance with classification searching. This is the most effective and time-efficient way to identify classification areas for a search.

Patent examiners are able to identify areas to search that are not entirely intuitive simply by reading the classification manual. Additionally, they are experts in their assigned technology areas, experts in using their assigned patent classes, and they can "translate" cryptic or ambiguous subclass names.

We recommend that you contact an examiner for each class that is relevant in your cursory search to identify classification areas. For the current example, the classes would be 340, 180, 307, 123, and 342.

Pay attention to subclasses that you notice repeatedly (ones that jump out at you) in your preliminary searching. Spend only a couple minutes looking up the subclass titles so you have an idea of the subject matter within them. Also remember the names of any primary examiners that have appeared frequently in the patents you identified during the preliminary search. This will help you in the next step.

Contact an examiner for each related class.

On the following USPTO employee locator page, search for art units by class ("Class/Subclass GAU Information" in the left column). Take note of the art units associated with each class as well as the corresponding ranges

of subclass and look up each appropriate art unit roster. Look over the ros-
ters for primary examiner names you noted in step 1 and call them first. If
they are not available, call anyone in the art unit.

If you are unsure who would be appropriate to contact in an art unit,
say: "Hello, my name is _____, and I am a public searcher. Can you direct
me to someone who can assist me with a search in class _____?"

Otherwise, call a primary examiner directly and ask him or her for help
with a search in the corresponding class. When he or she agrees, describe
the invention briefly and let them know what features of the invention you
are hoping to find in that particular class. The examiner will provide you
with a list of subclasses and usually will let you know what you can expect
to find in each one.

IPC (International Patent Classification)   The IPC is an internationally
uniform classification of patent documents. Its primary purpose is to serve
as an effective search tool for the retrieval of patent documents by patent
offices and other users, in order to establish the novelty and evaluate the inventive step (including the assessment of technical advance and useful results or utility) of patent applications.

The classification symbol is made up of a letter denoting the IPC section,
followed by a number (two digits) denoting the IPC class (e.g., B62). Optionally, the classification can be followed by a sequence of a letter (e.g.,
B62J) denoting the IPC subclass, a number (variable, 1 to 3 digits, e.g.,
B62J11) denoting the IPC main group, a forward slash ("/") and a number
(variable, 1 to 3 digits, e.g., B62J11/00) denoting the IPC subgroup.

To obtain the classes and subclasses using IPC for foreign searches,
known U.S. classes and subclasses are converted to IPC classes and subclasses by using the "US-to-IPC Concordance" issued by the USPTO.
This tool is an approximation and should not be relied upon exclusively.
An online version is available at the USPTO Web site: www.uspto.gov/
web/patents/classification/.

As a quick example, finding the IPC concordance for U.S. subclass
180/287 yields B60R 25/00:

PERFORMING OPERATIONS TRANSPORTING; VEHICLES IN
GENERAL; VEHICLES, VEHICLE FITTINGS, OR VEHICLE PARTS,
NOT OTHERWISE PROVIDED FOR; Vehicle fittings for preventing or
indicating unauthorized use or theft of vehicles

Upon reviewing B60R 25/00 in the IPC schedule, it becomes apparent that the more specific B60R 25/10 is also relevant as it pertains to ". . . actuating a signaling device."

Another method of obtaining IPC classes and subclasses is to examine the IPC schedule, which is also available online (http://cxp.paterra.com/). The IPC class and subclasses can be obtained by placing the subject matter that is being searched into appropriate class and subclass definitions on the IPC schedule.

ECLA (European Patent Office Classification)   The ECLA classification system is an extension of the IPC system. It contains 129,200 subdivisions (i.e., about 60,000 more than the IPC) and is more precise. It is also more homogeneous and more systematic. ECLA classifications are assigned to patent documents by European Patent Office (EPO) examiners in order to facilitate prior art searches. ECLA is revised continuously and applied retrospectively. Regarding ECLA notation, the EC subgroup may be added to the IPC symbol. It has the form of a letter, followed by a number (optional), a letter (optional), and so on (e.g., B62J11/00B).

FI/F-Term   The FI and F-Term systems were developed by the Japanese Patent Office (JPO) to classify Japanese patents. The file index or FI is the internal classification used by the JPO. It consists of an IPC subclass followed by a three-digit IPC subdivision symbol. The F-Term system was developed to parallel the IPC and the FI classification systems. Under the F-Term system, subject matters are classified in multiple viewpoints or themes as opposed to only one viewpoint under IPC system. Additional information is available at Japan National Center for Industrial Property Information and Training (NCIPI): www.ipdl.ncipi.go.jp/homepg_e.ipdl.

Preparing Initial Text Queries   As discussed earlier, a search is a continual iterative learning process. Therefore, it is virtually impossible to generate one single set of text queries at the outset to use throughout a search and know that the search is exhaustive and complete. Your text queries should be modified as the search progresses. Even if you are intimately familiar with the technical subject matter of the invention, you will find instances of new or unconventional phraseology, a new use for the invention, and new structural variations in the prior art as you go along that you can use to guide your search. However, a few techniques can increase the effectiveness and efficiency of your search at the outset.

The fundamental types of text search operators in the more sophisticated search engines are as follows:

Boolean operators

Typically AND, OR, NOT.

For finding unions, intersections, and subtractions from data sets.

Proximity operators

Typically ADJ, NEAR, WITH, SAME.

For finding words within a defined perimeter of other words

Truncation limiters

Typically indicated by a character such as "$" or "★".

Most engines support back truncation, and some also support front truncation (variable number of characters at the front or back of a root word) for detecting varying derivatives of the same word.

To illustrate the importance of truncation operators, the following example shows the number of variations on the word *attach* and how different in meaning each variation can be.

ATTACH	
Verb	Attach
	Attached
	Attaching
	Reattach (Re-attach)
	Reattaching (Re-attaching)
	Reattached (Re-attached)
Noun	Attachment
Participle Adjective	Attaching Device
	Attaching Member
	Attaching Mechanism
Adjective	Attachable
Adverb	Attachable

The following table shows the most common text search operators, their purpose, and basic syntax.

Text Search Operators

Operator	Function	Syntax
AND	All terms in combination are in the document.	Term1 AND Term2
OR	One or the other or both terms are in the document.	Term1 OR Term2
XOR	One or the other but *not* both terms are in the document.	Term1 XOR Term2
NOT	One term is present and the other term is not in the document.	Term1 NOT Term2
ADJ	Terms appear in the order specified next to one another or within a prescribed number of words of one another.	Term1 ADJ Term2 Term1 ADJ3 Term2
NEAR	Terms appear in any order next to one another or within a prescribed number of words of one another.	Term1 NEAR Term2 Term1 NEAR5 Term2
WITH	Terms appear in the same sentence.	Term1 WITH Term2
SAME	Terms appear in the same paragraph.	Term1 SAME Term2
"*" "$" "?"	Unlimited characters or a prescribed number of characters in front (left truncation) or behind (right truncation) the term.	Automo* (automotive or automobile) *motive (locomotive) Automa*4 (auto-mation, but NOT automatically)

Using these operators and our invention diagram template shown earlier, the keywords that were generated by brainstorming can be formed into a few examples of initial search queries as shown in the following table.

Problem			(police or (law adj enforcement)) with (chas*4 or pursu*3)
Solution	What it is: (structure)	Control Module	(control or module or terminal or computer or console) and ((identif*7 or locat*4 or determin*3 or match*3 or choos*3 or select*3 or find*3) with (vehicle*1 or car*1 or truck*1 or automobile*1)) and (police or (law adj enforcement))

Transmitter	((radio or RF or infrared or IR or ultrasonic or (wi adj fi) or Bluetooth or satellite or laser) with (transmit*5 or send*4 or signal*4 or messag*3 or data)) same (vehicle*1 or car*1 or truck*1 or automobile*1) same ((law adj enforcement) or police or pursu*3)
Receiver	((radio or RF or infrared or IR or ultrasonic or (wi adj fi) or Bluetooth or satellite) with (receiv*3 or reception or signal*4 or messag*3 or data)) same (vehicle*1 or car*1 or truck*1 or automobile*1)
Valve	(valve or restrict*3)
Switch	(switch or relay or break*3)
What it does: (function)	(disabl*5 or imped*4 or block*3 or prevent*4 or inhibit*3 or restrict*3 or stop*4) and (vehicle or car or truck or automobile)
	(((cut*4 or shut*4 or turn*3) adj off) or cutoff or shutoff or disconnect*3 or break*3) with ((fuel adj (pump or line or inject*3)) or ignition or distributor or spark or plug or wire or batter*3 or power or electric*3 or circuit) and (vehicle*1 or car*1 or truck*1 or automobile*1)

In these examples, the asterisk "*" is used as the wildcard for truncation limiting and it is assumed that the search engine does not automatically account for plurals. Search engines that consider plurals automatically do not require truncation limiters for "s", "es", or "ies" at the end of words. It is important to note how some of these strings are constructed. To account for all of the variations in which a device could discontinue the flow of fuel, consider the following string:

(((cut*4 or shut*4 or turn*4) adj off) or cutoff or
shutoff or disconnect*3 or break*3)

Using the "adj" (adjacent) command, the string accounts for words like "cut off" and variations including "cut-off", "cutoff", and "cutting off." Likewise, there are several different pieces of equipment in a vehicle that handle the fuel. Any of these pieces of equipment could be affected by the cutoff mechanism. The following string accounts for this dilemma:

(fuel adj (pump or line or inject*3))

The string anticipates that the fuel pump, a fuel line, or the fuel *injectors* or fuel *injection* may be cut off or blocked.

The two preceding examples are grouped together using a "with" command to specify that these phrases will occur in the same sentence. Such a sentence could be:

"It is therefore desirable to cut off the fuel pump to stall the engine."

At this stage you have comprehensively prepared for a search by scoping the subject matter and dissecting the invention into discrete, searchable subject features. You have established a thorough set of initial classification areas to search, and you developed initial text search queries. With these tools, you have a solid and clearly defined angle of attack. You are ready to begin.

CONDUCTING THE SEARCH

There are two primary factors that separate an experienced patent searcher from a novice searcher: the ability to quickly find the best patent documents and the ability to accurately assess the relevancy of each patent document reviewed. This section of the chapter addresses both of these functions in discussing not only the mechanics involved in conducting a search, but perhaps more importantly, what a professional patent searcher thinks during his or her evaluation of a single patent document. Literally speaking, a patent search is reviewing one patent document after another within a result set and determining how much each document is related to the subject matter at hand. This applies whether the result set is from a pure text search, a classification search, a combined text and classification search, or the backward or forward citations of a single document. It is one thing to know the steps required for a thorough and complete search, but they are meaningless without the tools to know which documents to select and which not to select for your final deliverable. Beyond evaluating patent documents, this chapter discusses how to strategically, and therefore efficiently, approach classification searching and full-text searching as well as a number of considerations regarding patent citations.

Evaluating Patent Documents

When determining the relevancy of a patent document during a search, a patent searcher will essentially do two things: screen the appropriate parts of the patent for information needed to determine its relevancy to the search, and determine which discrete subject features that the invention in hand and the document being reviewed have in common.

The Sections of a Patent and Their Usefulness in Patent Searching

Patent documents have perfectly predictable formats and all contain virtually the same information: bibliographic information (title, abstract, inventor(s), assignee(s), filing date, priority date, priority document information, citations, etc.), a specification including a detailed description of the invention, claims, and drawings if applicable. Patent formats vary from one patenting authority to another, but they all are arranged to show the same basic information. This is to your advantage whether you are searching patent images or abbreviated patent content as often supplied by many search engines.

Beyond the "Description of the Invention," which is found in the patent specification, the patent searcher will primarily study four other sections of a patent document to determine relevancy: (1) Title, (2) Abstract, (3) Claims, and (4) Drawings.

Titles   Patent titles provide the least reliable clues for determining the relevancy of a patent. This is because titles vary from the very descriptive to intentionally vague. However, patent titles are relatively short and can be searched quickly. A search by title within a patent class is an effective approach for identifying *potentially* relevant documents. It is quick because only the title is read; and reliable because the titles are searched within a class of similar patents. A professional search requires more than a search of patent titles.

Abstracts   Abstracts provide summaries of claimed inventions and point to the most novel embodiments. It is possible that some of the keywords used in a text search will appear in the abstract, but more likely an abstract will provide an overall sense of the invention. As with titles, abstracts are relatively easy to read and can help identify *potentially* relevant documents. A professional search requires more than a search of patent abstracts.

Descriptions of the Invention   With most searches, your objective is to locate the prior art references that address specific subject features. Every claimed embodiment of the invention and its recited subject features must be addressed and supported in the description part of the specification.[2] Therefore, your careful reading of the specification will reveal much about the relevancy of the patent reference to the subject matter at hand.

Claims   The patent applicant must disclose the novelty or inventive step of an invention in the claims.[3] By reading the claims, you can determine the scope of the patent; however, the claims may be directed to only one embodiment, method, or article and might not recite subject features addressed in the specification. Typically, claims language is merely descriptive. Although claims may assist you in determining the relevancy of the patent reference, the reading of them for patentability is less helpful than searching the patent specification for relevancy. With infringement or clearance, however, claims must read to assess relevancy.

Drawings   Drawings can show and reveal features central to the focus of the search that are not described or even addressed in other parts of the patent. You should search the drawings in technical fields where images are essential to the description of the invention. This is true, for example, in the mechanical arts.

You may want to search drawings when the technological field is crowded with many patents. Image searching improves your efficiency because most people can "flip through" drawings faster than they can read text. When finding subject features of interest, the documents should be marked for further review to determine their relevancy to the search. A professional search requires more than a review of drawings. Drawings will not uncover all possible variations in materials or components that may be important to the search.

Determining Relevancy According to the Invention Subject Features
If you were to watch a professional patent searcher review a stack of patents for relevancy, you would notice that he or she spends very little time, perhaps a couple of seconds, looking at some of them but several minutes looking at others. Additionally, you might notice that the searcher can get through a large number of documents in a surprisingly short amount of time. It is clear that the searcher does not read every document from front

to back. Then what decision-making process is going on that enables the searcher to appropriately separate the documents between ones to keep and ones to throw away? This decision-making process is at the absolute epicenter of patent searching and takes time and practice to develop. In time this skill becomes automatic.

This process can be best explained by a hierarchical decision tree. By using any combination of the parts of a patent document, the searcher decides first whether very core features of the invention being searched are met. If so, the searcher then investigates the document in more detail to check for the next most important features, and so on. If not, the document is excluded from the search results and not reviewed again. Depending on the technology involved in the search, the searcher may start with the title, then move to the abstract, then the claims, then the specification. Alternatively, the searcher may start with the drawings and then go straight to the specification to look up parts labeled by drawing numbers to see how they are discussed. Regardless of the mechanics, the searcher will be looking to make decisions about what the document contains in generally the same fashion. We will use the feature map in Exhibit 3.1 as a pictorial representation of this decision-making process.

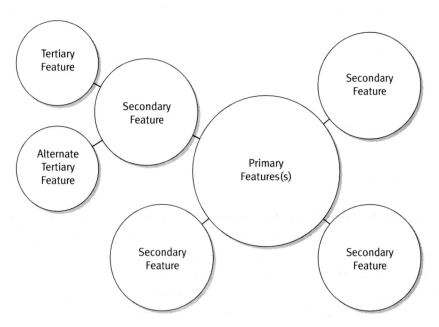

E X H I B I T   3 . I   Feature Map

To revisit the vehicle disablement sample invention, a map of the features discussed by the invention disclosure may look like Exhibit 3.2.

The central features are of critical importance to the decision-making process in evaluating patent documents, and it is important to make certain they are accurate. These features are the first criteria in the decision-making process, and if they are misaligned, the entire search will be skewed. They must be sufficiently specific and sufficiently broad at the same time.

- **Remote:** All patent documents uncovered during the search must show disablement systems that operate remotely. The searcher will not be interested in systems that disable the engine internally, for example, when an impact is detected.

- **Vehicle:** The word *vehicle* can mean many things, from an automobile to a motorcycle to an aircraft. Although the sample invention pertains to automobiles, disablement systems for other vehicles may have similar components or operations.

- **Disablement:** The system must disable the vehicle and not simply slow it down or mildly impede progress. Other security systems may limit but still allow fuel flow, may limit engine speed, or apply the brakes.

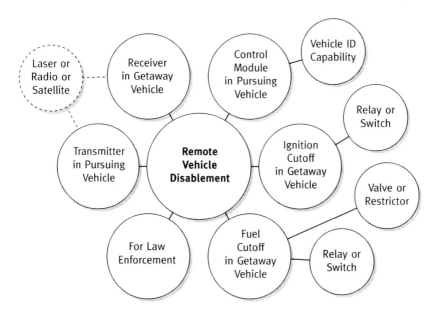

E X H I B I T   3 . 2   **Invention Disclosure**

Take note of the alternate features for the fuel cutoff mechanism in that the system can be a valve/restrictor or a relay/switch. Also note the dashed feature, "Laser or radio or satellite," which describes how the wireless components communicate with one another. While the invention description for the sample invention was not specific in this regard, this hypothetical feature illustrates how two components can be bridged by necessity. To communicate properly, two wireless communication devices must use the same communication medium.

When reviewing individual documents, this feature map can be used as a checklist. Consider two of the patents found in the initial scoping queries earlier in this chapter and their associated feature maps (see Exhibits 3.3 and 3.4).

Upon review of the title, it appears that the document is on point. However, it is impossible to tell how the system functions from the title alone. The abstract provides more detail:

> *A method of and system for enabling pursuing police cruisers or the like to remotely and safely stop the engine of an appropriately equipped stolen or improperly operated vehicle, wherein the cruiser transmits a control signal to a receiver pre-provided in the vehicle, to initiate, preferably through modified engine control modules, a forced and over-riding multiple-stage reduction in fuel supplied to the engine, first to slow down the vehicle below idling speed, and then to stall the engine by total fuel shut off.*

It is still unclear from the abstract how the fuel shutoff works. From Exhibits 3.3 and 3.4, we learn that the fuel shutoff is achieved electrically by controlling the electric fuel pump. There is no mention in the document of fuel flow restriction or cutoff.

Reviewing the patent reveals that it discusses both fuel cutoff and ignition cutoff. The patent also equips the pursuing law enforcement vehicle with a control module. However, it is not used for vehicle identification purposes. The control module is used for user authentication where biometric comparison matches the fingerprints of the user with those stored in a database. This feature is not required by the sample invention.

There is no universal approach to evaluating patent references for relevancy or for prioritizing them. However, you will save time and improve your productivity by creating a method that simplifies your work. It may be the mere listing of the more "important" patent numbers on a notepad as you search. It may be a worksheet that lists the subject features important

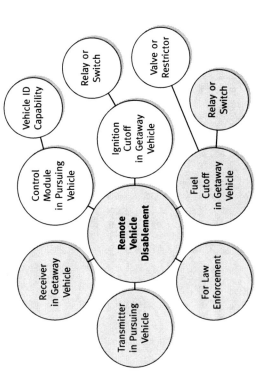

United States Patent [19]

Muise et al.

US006072248A

[11] Patent Number: 6,072,248

[45] Date of Patent: Jun. 6, 2000

[54] METHOD OF AND SYSTEM FOR EXTERNALLY AND REMOTELY DISABLING STOLEN OR UNAUTHORIZED OPERATED VEHICLES BY PURSUING POLICE AND THE LIKE

[76] Inventors: Christopher Russel Muise, 26 Campmeeting Rd., Topsfield, Mass. 01983; Daniel Grant Thomas, 360 Winter St., North Andover, Mass. 01845

[21] Appl. No.: 09/129,734

[22] Filed: Aug. 5, 1998

[51] Int. Cl.7 .... B60R 25/04
[52] U.S. Cl. 307/10.2; 180/287; 340/825.72
[58] Field of Search .... 307/10.1, 10.2, 10.3-10.6; 340/426, 425.5, 825.06, 825.69, 825.72, 825.3-825.32, 825.34, 901, 902, 904; 342/44; 123/333, 198 DB

[56]   References Cited
            U.S. PATENT DOCUMENTS

4,878,050 10/1989 Kelley 340/426
5,559,491   9/1996 Stadler 340/426
5,861,799   1/1999 Szwed 307/10.2

Primary Examiner—Richard T. Elms
Attorney, Agent, or Firm—Rines and Rines

[57]   ABSTRACT

A method of and system for enabling pursuing police cruisers or the like to remotely and safely stop the engine of an appropriately equipped stolen or improperly operated vehicle, wherein the cruiser transmits a control signal to a receiver pre-provided in the vehicle, to initiate, preferably through modified engine control modules, a forced and over-riding multiple-stage reduction in fuel supplied to the engine, first to slow down the vehicle below idling speed, and then to stall the engine by total fuel shut off.

20 Claims, 6 Drawing Sheets

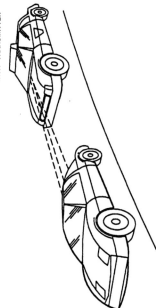

POLICE CRUISER WITH TRANSMITTER

EXHIBIT 3.3   u.s. 6,072,248

Vehicle ID Capability

Relay or Switch

Valve or Restrictor

Relay or Switch

Control Module in Pursuing Vehicle

Ignition Cutoff in Getaway Vehicle

Fuel Cutoff in Getaway Vehicle

Receiver in Getaway Vehicle

Remote Vehicle Disablement

For Law Enforcement

Transmitter in Pursuing Vehicle

US006411217B1

(12) **United States Patent**
Gabbard

(10) Patent No.: **US 6,411,217 B1**
(45) Date of Patent: **Jun. 25, 2002**

(54) **VEHICLE DISABLING SYSTEM**

(76) Inventor: **Charles H. Gabbard**, P.O. Box 7952, Newport Beach, CA (US) 92658

(*) Notice: Subject to any disclaimer, the term of this patent is extended or adjusted under 35 U.S.C. 154(b) by 0 days.

(21) Appl. No.: 09/517,892

(22) Filed: Mar. 3, 2000

Related U.S. Application Data

(63) Continuation-in-part of application No. 09/159,438, filed on Sep. 24, 1998, now Pat. No. 6,124,805, which is a continuation-in-part of application No. 09/081,475, filed on May 19, 1998, now Pat. No. 6,232,884.

(51) Int. Cl.⁷ G06F 7/04
(52) U.S. Cl. 340/825.31; 340/425.5; 340/426, 180/287; 307/9.1; 307/10.2
(58) Field of Search 340/825.31, 825.69, 340/825.72, 425.5, 426; 341/176; 180/287; 307/9.1, 10.2

(56) **References Cited**

U.S. PATENT DOCUMENTS

4,001,822 A	1/1977	Sterzer	
4,660,528 A	4/1987	Buck	
4,878,050 A	10/1989	Kelley	
5,006,661 A	4/1991	Raj	
5,293,527 A	3/1994	Dixon	
5,533,589 A	7/1996	Coitze	
5,588,038 A	12/1996	Snyder	
5,917,405 A	* 6/1999	June	340/426
5,933,075 A	* 8/1999	Ditson	180/287
6,072,248 A	* 6/2000	Muise et al	307/10.2
6,140,939 A	* 10/2000	Flick	340/825.31

OTHER PUBLICATIONS

Lanier Technology Inc. "Beyond a Shadow of A Doubt . . ." LTT 28–20, four pages No Page #'s.

* cited by examiner

Primary Examiner—Timothy Edwards, Jr.
(74) Attorney, Agent, or Firm—Stetina Brunda Garred & Brucker

(57) **ABSTRACT**

A vehicle disabling system for terminating operation of a vehicle. The system includes a transmit unit for transmitting a command shutdown message and a command-receiver vehicle unit within the subject vehicle or communication with at least one operational component of the vehicle and capable of shutting down that component to thereby terminate vehicle operation. The transmit unit is operable only by an operator having a pre-authorized biometrics identification that is read, recognized, and confirmed by the transmit unit site prior to system activation. Both the transmit unit and the vehicle unit preferably are in separate communication with the global positioning satellite. With respect to the transmit unit, such satellite communication functions to record all transmit unit usage to thereby maintain and assure proper and appropriate operator use thereof. With respect to the vehicle unit, such satellite communication functions to receive location information of the vehicle both for apprehension purposes and for stolen-vehicle recovery purposes. Use of the system can ensure reduced risk and danger to innocent third parties as well as to law enforcement personnel by essentially eliminating the need for vehicle chases.

18 Claims, 1 Drawing Sheet

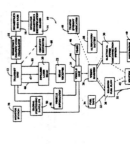

U.S. 6,411,217

EXHIBIT 3.4

to the search and the searcher's notations about which sections of patents he reads that are the same or similar to the subject features under consideration. We recommend the latter.

The worksheet can be created by converting the feature map into a *feature matrix*. The feature matrix serves three purposes: (1) to capture your assessment as you read the reference, (2) to give you a tool to map which sections of the prior art reference need further review, and (3) to create an objective tool for determining which patent reference is most similar to the subject matter under consideration (i.e., most subject features represented).

First, the following feature matrix for the sample invention simply indicates which features are present in each document uncovered. This can be a tool that you have in front of you as you search to very quickly mark off features as you read them.

	Remote Vehicle Disablement	For law enforcement	Transmitter in pursuing vehicle	Receiver in getaway vehicle	Control Module in pursuing vehicle	Vehicle ID capability	Ignition cutoff in getaway vehicle	Ignition cutoff: relay or switch	Fuel cutoff in getaway vehicle	Fuel cutoff: valve or restrictor	Fuel cutoff: relay or switch	No. of Subject Features Represented
U.S. 6,072,248	X	X	X	X					X		X	6
U.S. 6,411,217	X	X	X	X	X		X		X	X		8

To take this a step further, instead of simply indicating which features are discussed in each document, notes can be made to show where in each document the features are discussed. This helps tremendously when assembling a report, but can be more time consuming.

	Subject Feature 1	Subject Feature 2	Subject Feature 3	No. of Subject Features Represented
U.S. 7,000,000	Claim 1		Column 3 Line 40	2
U.S. 7,000,001		Claims 1 and 4	1	
U.S. 7,000,002	Claims 5 and 11		Drawing Figure 1 (a)	2

Evaluating Patent Documents in Different Search Types

Patentability and Validity as Applied to 35 United States Code (USC) § 102 and 103   In both patentability and validity searches, the objective is to find prior art references that either (a) anticipate the disclosed/claimed invention or (b) render the disclosed/claimed inventive subject matter of the search as being obvious to a person of ordinary skill in the art at the time of invention. In the United States, patentability is defined in 35 USC § 102 and 35 USC § 103.

An anticipatory reference, also known as a USC 102 reference, is one that addresses all subject features of a disclosed/claimed invention. Such a reference, if discovered in a patentability or validity search, would mean that the disclosed/claimed invention is not novel. Therefore, a relevant USC 102 anticipatory reference addresses all features of all levels (1 through 4) of the *Hierarchy of Criteria for Determining Relevancy* presented earlier in this chapter.

A USC 103 obviousness reference, on the other hand, is one that teaches one or more but not all subject features of a disclosed/claimed invention. A primary USC 103 reference addresses a majority of "critical" features of levels 1 through 3 of the hierarchy of criteria and, possibly, some of the more narrowly limiting features of level 4. Secondary USC 103 references are those that teach one or more subject features that are not addressed in the primary USC 103 references. A claimed invention can be rejected as obvious over a primary USC 103 reference in view of a secondary USC 103 reference and appropriate motivation provided for a person skilled in the art.[4] As such, a strongly relevant USC 103 obviousness reference is the type of a primary reference used in a USC 103 rejection of a patent claim. All secondary USC 103 reference-type documents identified in a search are relevant USC 103 references; however, any relevant USC 103 reference that teaches at least one inventive subject feature that is not taught in any other located references must also be considered as a strongly relevant USC 103 secondary reference that must be selected.

Therefore, you should attempt to locate patent references that address, in combination with other such references, all of the subject features of the disclosed/claimed invention. The patent searcher or patent information specialist should find the art and the attorney or patent agent should assess the applicability of each document to anticipation, obviousness, and motivation.

A professional search will provide a patent attorney with technological insights, and will support his or her legal assessments. We caution that a professional legal opinion should be provided only by a qualified patent attorney. A legal opinion should not be sought from or provided by a patent searcher.

Identifying the Subject Features for a Patentability Search In order to search for patentability, you need to know the salient features of the invention ("subject features") and why they are novel ("points of novelty"). Sometimes you can infer, from an invention disclosure, what these features are and why they are novel. If not, you should speak to the inventor before executing the search. The reason is simple. The salient features will determine the scope of the search. The scope of the search will determine your search strategy and how you assess the relevancy of the resulting references. The relevancy of the references will determine its usefulness in arriving at an eventual legal position.

Identifying the Subject Features for a Validity Search You will find the subject features of a validity search in the embodiments of an invention, as claimed in the granted patent. Embodiments are written in the claims in a way that defines the invention.

Claims must be read intently to understand their scope, for they are carefully written with words and phrases that are "descriptively rigorous." The claims establish the exact legal protection sought by the applicant and agreed to by the patent office. In fact, in the United States the patent applicant is permitted to be his own lexicographer; he can create and define the meanings of the words used in his application.[5] Therefore, you will need to carefully study the claims when executing the validity search.

The most relevant references, in either case, are those that address the largest number of identified subject features of the subject matter of the search. The best references are USC 102 references because "novelty" is less prone to interpretation than "obviousness." Nevertheless, USC 103 references will constitute the majority of references discovered in a search. To prepare for further relevancy evaluation and final selection, the marked potentially relevant documents must first be grouped into USC 102, 103 primary (strongly relevant), and strongly relevant USC 103 secondary references (as described earlier). This requires recording subject features addressed in a document when (at the same time) marking a document as a potentially relevant reference. A table and/or map can then be used to list the documents and subject features they address, ranked and categorized as described. For a validity/invalidity search, claims of interest and their recited claim interests are mapped to references and addressed as well.

Many patent attorneys prefer to review the strongly relevant references found in a search prior to less relevant references. Therefore, we recommend that you report the results of the search in this order: all USC 102 references followed by all strongly relevant USC 103 references. The strongly relevant 103 primary references will address the largest number of subject features.

Identifying the Subject Features for an Infringement Search   The purpose of an infringement search is to locate unexpired (in-force) patents whose claims "read on" the subject features of the search. Therefore, an infringement search requires the searching and reading of the claims of potentially relevant in-force patents. In United States infringement cases, the claims should be interpreted with deference to the written description of the invention.[6]

The patent information specialist's understanding of patent laws is most useful to an infringement search. Consider the following example of how the use of one word will impact the relevancy of a patent reference: when the subject matter of an infringement search *comprises* features A, B, and C; an in-force patent claiming a subject matter *comprising* features A, B, C, and D reads on the subject matter of the search and the patent is relevant (see Exhibit 3.5). But, an in-force patent that claims a subject matter *consisting of* features A, B, C, and D is not relevant.[7]

Unless you are a patent attorney, it is better to report patent references to the qualified attorney who is writing the legal opinion than to exclude them for fear that they may not be relevant. Not reporting the reference could deprive the legal practitioner of a potentially important document.[8]

Identifying the Subject Features for a Clearance or Freedom to Operate Search   Clearance searches (sometimes known as "Freedom to Operate" or "Right to Use" searches) differ from infringement searches. They require a search of both unexpired and expired patents. The reason for including a search of expired patents is that expired patents are freely avail-

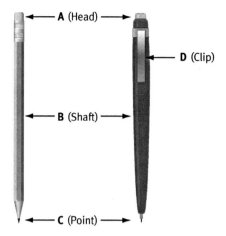

For instance, when the writing utensil of an infringement search comprises features **A, B,** and **C**; a live patent claiming a subject matter comprising features **A, B, C** and **D** reads on the subject matter of the search and the patent is relevant. However, a live patent that claims a subject matter consisting of features **A, B, C,** and **D** is not relevant.

E X H I B I T   3 . 5   Comprises Versus Consisting Of

able to the public. Thomas Edison's incandescent lamp may not be patented a second time. Therefore, anyone would be "clear" to make, use, and sell the products or services that depend on that expired, patented technology.

Individuals, companies, and other organizations commission clearance searches in order to protect themselves prior to making, using, or selling a new product or service. They want to identify any possible claim of infringement against them prior to their investment.

Classification Searching

Patent classification systems (PCSs) provide for storage and retrieval of every patent document in the possession of a patent granting office. A PCS is a hierarchical system for cataloging and indexing every patent document in a patent granting office into divisions/subdivisions, groups/subgroups, categories/subcategories, and classes/subclasses; the class is defined by a title, a definition, and a code. Each class in a patent classification system is intended to define a broad technological area. Subclasses further define the technology more narrowly.

With the advent of electronic documentation technology, a searcher may now perform a "text" search of the subject features of the subject matter of the search and to locate relevant documents without visiting a patent office or searching classes or subclasses.

However, a professional search requires more than text searching. A systematic and exhaustive search of "core" and "peripheral" subclasses is imperative to a *reliable* search. We recommend that every search include both text and classification searching (see Exhibit 3.6).

Core Classification Searching   Classes and subclasses most closely related to the subject matter constitute the core classification areas of a search. The most relevant patent documents due to their core structural features or functions are classified in core subclasses. They should be searched thoroughly and each patent document read individually for its relevancy.[9]

Class 600 — SURGERY

This Class 600 is considered to be an integral part of Class 128.

300	• DIAGNOSTIC TESTING
301	• Via monitoring a plurality of physiological data, e.g., pulse and blood pressure
302	• Endoradiosonde
303	• Olfactometer
304	• Readiness to give birth
305	• Hazardous current flow conditions
306	• Measurement of skin parameters
307	• Determining rate of fluid los from the body surface
308	• Physical characteristics of electrolytes
309	• Measuring or detecting nonradioactive constituent of body liquid by means placed against or in body throughout test
310	• Infrared, visible light, or ultraviolet radiation directed on or through body

E X H I B I T   3 . 6   **U.S. Class and Subclassification Example**

For instance, in the United States Patent Classification System,[10] Class 375—PULSE OR DIGITAL COMMUNICATIONS—defines an area in the electrical art that includes circuits, devices, methods, processes, and systems that "use electrical or electromagnetic signals for communication; including transmitting an intelligence bearing signal from one point to another in the form of discrete variations in some parameter of the electrical or electromagnetic signal." Subclass 130—SPREAD SPECTRUM—further limits Class 375 to a "subject matter utilizing a data modulated signal which has its energy spread over a transmitted bandwidth which is much greater than the bandwidth or rate of information being sent."

Further limitations narrow the definition of the subject matter of a subclass to more narrowly defined subclasses. The PTO classification system indents the narrower subclass under its parent subclass. Subclass 132—FREQUENCY HOPPING, and subclass 138—TIME HOPPING, for example, are indented under Subclass 130, with further narrowed definitions: "subject matter including a system in which the wide band signal is generated by jumping from one frequency to another over multiple number of frequency choices" and "subject matter including a system wherein waveforms are transmitted at times which are selected from among a plurality of time slots, with the selection of time slot being pseudo-random, if desired," respectively.

Transmitters and receivers are basic and integral parts of any communication systems. However, these basic but general subject matters could be classified in different subclasses, based on any additional limiting features. For instance, receivers—with the general functionality definition "comprising recovery, demodulation, and decoding of signals"—are classified in two subclasses, 136 and 147, based on the technology in which they are used (frequency hopping and direct sequence, respectively). And still, there are three subclasses, 148, 149, and 150, indented under subclass 147.[11]

Therefore, a patent claiming a receiver in a communication system that utilizes spread spectrum and direct sequence techniques is most likely classified in subclasses 147 and, possibly, any of subclasses 148 through 151 (subclass 151 is indented under 150). Core classification of this subject matter includes subclasses 147 through 151. If the definition of the claimed receiver also includes the subject matter of any of subclasses 148 through 151, then those subclasses should be considered as core classification; searching them would capture the most likely relevant patent documents.

As discussed earlier, core subclasses should be searched thoroughly and exhaustively. However, when there are core subclasses at different levels of hierarchy, common sense would seem to suggest that only the first subclass should be searched (because patents at lower subclasses are classified under upper/parent subclass). Due to different reasons, cross–classification and examiner's interpretation of the subject matter being just two, this is not so. As an example, at the time of writing this book, while there are 784 patent documents classified in U.S. subclass 375/147, 2,721 patent documents, with no duplications, are classified in subclasses 375/147–150! Therefore, all identified subclasses must be combed exhaustively in core classification searching.[12]

As a further example, upon revisiting the sample invention and our classification scoping in the previous section of this chapter, the core classification areas would most likely include the following:

- USPC: 180/287, 340/426.11, 340/426.13, 307/10.2, 123/333, 123/335
- IPC: B60R 25/10

Since core areas are those that will pertain to the core features of the invention, these all relate to vehicle disablement. Even though the classes represented include MOTOR VEHICLES (180), ELECTRICAL COMMUNICATIONS (340), ELECTRICAL TRANSMISSION (307), and INTERNAL COMBUSTION ENGINES (123), all of these classes have subclasses specifying some form of vehicle disablement. Note that none of the preceding subclasses pertain to the subfeatures of the invention.

Peripheral Classification Searching   Peripheral classification areas are those areas that have to do with subfeatures or subfunctions of the invention. A subject feature of an invention may include subfeatures or subfunctions that may be classified in arts analogous to the primary technological area. Depending on your available time and budget, it may or may not be practical to search these peripheral classes as thoroughly as you have searched the core areas. However, it is wise to at least search within the peripheral areas using carefully limiting text strings. Limit the peripheral subclasses by only one cluster of keywords at a time.

The most pertinent subclasses identified for any search should be exhaustively combed to the extent that every patent document classified within them is reviewed. However, patent documents are classified using a variety of criteria. Two patents having similar physical structural features may be classified in entirely different areas if they have markedly different uses. Likewise, the reverse is true. Although the USPTO recommends that independent inventors rely heavily on the classification system, classification searching cannot be relied upon exclusively to ensure that all relevant documents are considered.

Again, to revisit our sample invention, peripheral classification areas might include the following:

- U.S. 180/283, 180/284, 340/825.69, 340/825.72, 340/902, 340/904, 340/426.1, 340/5.2, 340/426.16, 340/426.17, 307/9.1, 342/44, 123/332, 123/334
- IPC: B60R 25/00

For example subclass 180/283 pertains to interrupting the ignition circuit of a vehicle's engine. At first glance, this appears particularly important. However, note that subclass 283 falls under 282, which pertains to actions that take place in response to sensing acceleration, deceleration, or tilt of a vehicle (i.e., an accident). While the actual mechanisms that interrupt the ignition of a vehicle that fall within 283 may be of interest during the search, they are intended for an entirely different application. Therefore, 180/283 is listed as peripheral.

Discrepancies in the U.S. Patent Classification System The numbered classification system used by the USPTO is best understood by the examiners at the USPTO. Consequently, you should always contact one or more examiners to clarify the classes you have chosen to search and to ensure that there are not other subclasses that you may not have considered.

Classification of patents is never cut and dried. In order to search through the clutter of overlapping classes you must have experience and patience. For example, if you were to begin searching for a flexible catheter and start in Class 604—"Surgery," as you browse down a page of subclasses you would begin to notice something strange. Subclass 264—"Body inserted tubular conduit structure"—fits the definition perfectly, as does 523—"Flexible catheter or means used therewith." You may decide to define the target invention better, but still flexible catheters exist in both. Overlapping subclasses present a hurdle for the patent information scientist;

and the numbers of patents that need review can increase dramatically. A search of U.S. patents in 604/264 (at the time of writing) contains over 1,500 patents, whereas 604/523 contains almost 1,000. By combining these and taking out the duplicates, this number reaches above 2,200.

Sorting through this many patents is inefficient without a careful strategy; and experience and organization play a key role in the ability to save valuable time when performing a search by not only avoiding duplicate searches but systematically breaking down where to place your resources during the search.

Full-Text Searching

Text searching is essentially a game of broadening and narrowing. It is important to have a strategic approach to text searching instead of haphazardly entering keywords into a search engine. Returning for a moment to some fundamentals at the beginning of this chapter, every invention is usually *one* solution to *one* problem. But the results of a comprehensive search will include documents showing several solutions to the same problem as well as documents showing similar inventions intended for completely different problems. A quandary that plagues patent searchers is: How do you find all of the possible alternate solutions to a single problem, and how do you find alternate problems with the same solution?

Use systematic text query progression. Text query progression is a way of attacking the subject matter of a search from several directions:

- Start with the generic structure or function (broad) and combine text queries gradually to include the problem (narrow).
- Start with the generic problem (broad) and combine text queries gradually to include the structure or function (narrow).
- Start with the problem, structure, and function combined (very narrow), and subtract keyword groupings to work outward. This method requires subtracting the result sets from each previous query to avoid redundancy.

An inherent flaw in using a text search progression in only one direction is that alternate structural or functional solutions to the same problem will not be detected. Likewise, alternate problems for the same structural components or function will not be detected. It is therefore recommended to use text search progressions in more than one direction. Consider the following scenarios using the sample invention:

Scenario 1: An initial search for the generic structural components—transmitter, receiver, relay, control module—followed by a first narrowing search for vehicle disablement, followed by a second narrowing search for high-speed police chases, will not capture documents containing impeding systems that apply the vehicle brakes to keep the vehicle from moving.

Scenario 2: An initial search for high-speed police chases followed by a first narrowing search for vehicle disablement, followed by a second narrowing search for the structural components, will not capture documents containing fuel flow shutoffs used for driver/occupant safety reasons.

Of course, patent documents discussing automatic braking systems or safety fuel shutoffs may or may not be relevant, depending on the required breadth of search.

It is important to study how text query progression affects search results by revisiting the preliminary search queries drafted earlier in this chapter.

Problem			(police or (law adj enforcement)) with (chas*4 or pursu*3)
Solution	What it is: (structure)	Control Module	(control or module or terminal or computer or console) and ((identif*7 or locat*4 or determin*3 or match*3 or choos*3 or select*3 or find*3) with (vehicle*1 or car*1 or truck*1 or automobile*1)) and (police or (law adj enforcement))
		Transmitter	((radio or RF or infrared or IR or ultrasonic or (wi adj fi) or Bluetooth or satellite or laser) with (transmit*5 or send*4 or signal*4 or messag*3 or data)) same (vehicle*1 or car*1 or truck*1 or automobile*1) same ((law adj enforcement) or police or pursu*3)
		Receiver	((radio or RF or infrared or IR or ultrasonic or (wi adj fi) or Bluetooth or satellite) with (receiv*3 or reception or signal*4 or messag*3 or data)) same (vehicle*1 or car*1 or truck*1 or automobile*1)

(continues)

Valve	(valve or restrict*3)
Switch	(switch or relay or break*3)
What it does: (function)	(disabl*5 or imped*4 or block*3 or prevent*4 or inhibit*3 or restrict*3 or stop*4) and (vehicle or car or truck or automobile)
	(((cut*4 or shut*4 or turn*3) adj off) or cutoff or shutoff or disconnect*3 or break*3) with ((fuel adj (pump or line or inject*3)) or ignition or distributor or spark or plug or wire or batter*3 or power or electric*3 or circuit) and (vehicle*1 or car*1 or truck*1 or automobile*1)

Now consider the following text search strategy.

Query	Hits	Criteria
1	220861	Full patent spec.: "(((cut*4 or shut*4 or turn*3) adj off) or cutoff or shutoff or disconnect*3 or break*3) with ((fuel adj (pump or line or inject*3)) or ignition or distributor or spark or plug or wire or batter*3 or power or electric*3 or circuit) and (vehicle*1 or car*1 or truck*1 or automobile*1)"
		Databases USG USA
		Years 1836–2006
2		Full patent spec.: "((radio or RF or infrared or IR or ultrasonic or (wi adj fi) or bluetooth or satellite or laser) with (transmit*5 or transmission or send*4 or receiv*3 or reception or signal*4 or messag*3 or data)) same (vehicle*1 or car*1 or truck*1 or automobile*1)"
		Databases USG USA
		Years 1836–2006
3	12930	Combine 1 and 2
4		Full patent spec.: "((valve or restrict*3 or reduc*3) with fuel) and ((switch*3 or relay or break*3) with (ignition or distributor))"
		Databases USG USA
		Years 1836–2006
5	231	Combine 3 and 4

This strategy starts with a specific recitation of the *function*, adds the *structural* text strings associated with the transmitter and receiver, and finally the broad *structural* text strings associated with the equipment used to cut the fuel and ignition. In other words, the strategy looks for anything that shuts off the fuel and ignition to a vehicle using a receiver, transmitter, valve, and switch. The strategy does not target law enforcement applications.

Consider a second search strategy.

Query	Hits	Criteria
1	66526	Full patent spec.: "((radio or RF or infrared or IR or ultrasonic or (wi adj fi) or bluetooth or satellite or laser) with (transmit*5 or transmission or send*4 or receiv*3 or reception or signal*4 or messag*3 or data)) same (vehicle*1 or car*1 or truck*1 or automobile*1)"
		Databases USG USA
		Years 1836–2006
2	459340	Full patent spec.: "(control or module or terminal or computer or console) and ((identif*7 or locat*4 or determin*3 or match*3 or choos*3 or select*3 or find*3) with (vehicle*1 or car*1 or truck*1 or automobile*1))"
		Databases USG USA
		Years 1836–2006
3	43224	Combine 1 and 2
4	2786	Full patent spec.: "(police or (law adj enforcement)) and (chas*4 or pursu*3)"
		Databases USG USA
		Years 1836–2006
5	705	Combine 3 and 4

This query begins with the *structural* text strings associated with the transmitter and receiver, adds *structural* text strings associated with the control module, and finally the *functional strings* to incorporate the law enforcement application. In other words, this strategy targets only the vehicle identification capability in the invention description for law enforcement officials to identify a particular vehicle from a control module using a transmitter and receiver between the vehicles. The strategy does not attempt to incorporate vehicle disablement.

The first example illustrates starting with the function alone and narrowing toward the structural components, whereas the second example begins with the structural components at the core of the invention and narrows toward the problem.

Citation Searching

There are two types of patent documents associated with most patents that can assist in a patent search.

Backward citations are patent documents and publications that are cited as references on the face of the subject patent. They were cited either by the patent examiner or the patent applicant during the examination process (also known as "patent prosecution").[13] *Forward citations* are patent documents and publications that were subsequently cited by other granted patents. You would need the help of a search engine to conduct a forward citation search, as these documents were cited after the patent was granted. Fortunately, most patent search engines allow users to conduct both backward and forward citation searching.

The citation search is useful for a few reasons. First, it is a search based on previous searches, either by the patent applicant and/or the examiner who granted a patent. It allows you to know how the invention was interpreted by the patent examiner and what technologies he or she considered relevant. It helps you to understand the examiner's thought process and how he or she defined the technology under examination.

When citation searching is continued to earlier or later patents (citation searches of cited references), you can begin to visualize the evolution of the technology. This iterative approach to citation searching over generations of patents is often fascinating.

For example, you may have found a patent in the same technical field that addresses the same problem as the invention you are searching for, but which does not meet the limitations of your target invention.

Citation searching could produce a large but related set of results, from which you might find a patent that meets the limitations of your target invention. The patent reference may be more relevant than the patent you found previously. Repeated searches might result in yet another patent that is even more closely related. When conducted systematically, citation searching often uncovers a tapestry of interwoven patents that gradually approach your desired result while enhancing your understanding of the field of the invention.

It is especially useful when you are not sure where to begin your search. You may know about your patent or just one patent of interest. By conducting a citation search you will gradually identify the evolution of the technology, terminology, and alternative search terms, and even terms that are unique to a specific invention.

By comparison, both classification and text searching presume that the searcher knows the terminology, synonyms, and equivalents of the technology, which he may not. If not, the quality of his search will suffer. Citation searches will improve his understanding of the art and allow him to adjust his search strategies accordingly.

Backward Citation Searching   Backward citation searching is often used to find the first fundamental discovery of a technology. Sometimes cited references are not on point when the examiner has been liberal in formulating rejections against the application during prosecution.

When choosing a patent to use as a starting point for a backward citation search, you should note the relevancy of the claims of the patent. Patent examiners base their search of a patent, and the references they cite in a patent, on what the patent claims. Therefore, if you find a patent having a disclosure with an embodiment that is somewhat close to what they are searching for, but this embodiment is not claimed, this patent may not be a good choice for a backward search. However, if the patent does claim a feature or features of the invention that is being searched for, then the patent examiner who issued the application also had to search for these features, and it is likely that he or she cited references relevant to these features.

Forward Citation Searching   In contrast to backward citation searching, when choosing a patent to use as a starting point for a forward citation search, it is important to emphasize the relevancy of the main embodiments of the patent disclosure rather than the claims (see Exhibit 3.7). An original patent that represents the first disclosure of a novel or unique feature will be a frequently cited source, regardless of whether this feature is claimed in the original patent. Therefore, finding a base patent that provides the fundamental disclosure of a particular technology can be a productive strategy when you are searching for an improvement of this particular technology.

Citations in both patents and journal articles can cite a never-ending chain of literature that can unearth both new inventions as well as a trail of

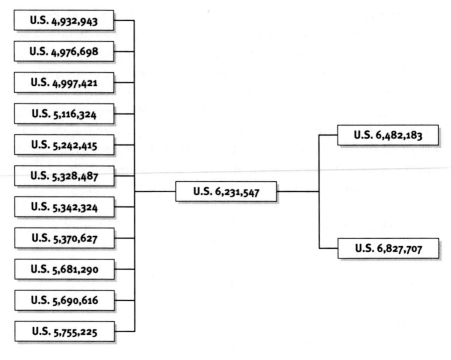

E X H I B I T   3 . 7   Sample Citation Tree

infringement. For example, if you find a paper that was published in 2001 that cites five references, as you dig deeper you will find that these five references each cite references of their own. This can quickly result in an exponential increase in prior art references that need to be reviewed.

Citation linking has long been a popular way to see an experiment or design develop. It offers an easy way to direct you as you search through prior art while also targeting key literature that may have highly important relevance. It should be noted, though, that an important reference may not be cited by the author if he deems it not relevant or is unaware that it exists.

Searching Foreign Patent Documents

It is imperative to all types of searches (except infringement) that a thorough foreign patent search be completed. Foreign art can be used to invalidate a troubled patent or render a new disclosure unpatentable. It is also important to know the foreign patent landscape for ensuring validity of your own patent.

Recent U.S. court decisions have shown the importance of locating as much of the relevant prior art as possible. In *In re Bruckelmeyer v. Ground Heaters* (U.S. Fed. Cir. 2006), the court found that a Canadian patent application obviated Bruckelmeyer's two patents, even though two drawings canceled during prosecution were needed to render the patents obvious. Bruckelmeyer argued unsuccessfully on appeal that the Canadian patent application was not a printed publication under 35 USC § 102(b) and this could not be construed as prior art. The Federal Circuit ruled that the original application was "publicly accessible" and therefore qualified as a prior art "printed publication" because the Canadian application's prosecution file was available to the public more than a year before the filing of the Bruckelmeyer applications.

Most patenting authorities utilize a different system than does the United States. An inventor who files an application in the United States has what is called a "grace period" of one year after the date of the public disclosure to file for a patent, while in many other countries a patent cannot be obtained if the invention was made public anywhere in the world even one day before the patent application was filed.

There are a number of different organizations and international agreements that aim to centralize the protection of intellectual property worldwide. It is important to understand the background of the authorities that generate the prior art that are searched outside of the United States.

Paris Convention for the Protection of International Property   The Paris Convention is the foundation upon which the rest of the world's collective intellectual property is built. It is the first significant international intellectual property treaty, signed in 1883 by 11 countries. The Paris Convention now has 169 contracting member countries, which makes it one of the most widely adopted treaties worldwide.[14]

The convention allows an applicant from one of the contracting states to use the first filing date in a member state as the effective filing date in another contracting state, provided the second application is filed no less than 12 months after the first.

The Paris Convention, like the Patent Cooperation Treaty (PCT), is administered by the World Intellectual Property Organization (WIPO). A country must be a signatory of the Paris Convention to be a signatory of the PCT.

The European Patent Organization   The European Patent Organization was established by the Convention on the Grant of European Patents (EPC)[15] signed in Munich on October 5, 1973. The EPC is a multilateral treaty incorporating the European Patent Organization,[16] providing an autonomous legal system by which European patents are granted. Once granted, a European patent becomes the equivalent to a patent in each of the designated (member) states. Each patent is singularly nationally enforceable or revocable in each member state. It is not a European-wide patent. The European Patent Organization has two main bodies: the Administrative Council, which is the legislative body, and the European Patent Office, which is the executive body.

The following countries are signatories to the EPC:

Austria (AT)	Ireland (IE)
Belgium (BE)	Iceland (IS)
Bulgaria (BG)	Italy (IT)
Switzerland (CH)	Liechtenstein (LI)
Cyprus (CY)	Lithuania (LT)
Czech Republic (CZ)	Luxembourg (LU)
Germany (DE)	Monaco (MC)
Denmark (DK)	Netherlands (NL)
Estonia (EE)	Poland (PL)
Spain (ES)	Portugal (PT)
Finland (FI)	Romania (RO)
France (FR)	Sweden (SE)
United Kingdom (GB)	Slovenia (SI)
Hellenic Republic (GR)	Slovakia (SK)
Hungary (HU)	Turkey (TR)

Extending states include Albania (AL), Bosnia and Herzegovina (BA), Croatia (HR), Latvia (LV), the former Yugoslav Republic of Macedonia (MK), and Serbia and Montenegro (YU).

The EPC is different from the European Union, and its membership is slightly different. Bulgaria, Iceland, Liechtenstein, Monaco, Romania, Switzerland, and Turkey[17] are signatories of the EPC, but are not members of the European Union (EU), and the opposite is true of Malta. The EPC provides a standardized legal framework for the granting of patents by way of a single homogenized process before the European Patent Office (EPO). A single application may be filed at one of the EPO's patent offices[18] or at the patent office of a contracting state if permitted by local law. While the

EPC allows for a quasi-judicial third-party opposition process, claims of infringement are settled by the laws of the national authority in which the claims are made.

World Intellectual Property Organization (WIPO)   WIPO was formally created in Stockholm, Sweden, by the Convention Establishing the World Intellectual Property Organization on July 14, 1967. The WIPO's mission is to "promote the protection of intellectual property rights around the world."[19] The WIPO currently has 183[20] member states and administers 23 international intellectual property treaties.

WIPO became a specialized agency of the United Nations in 1974. The WIPO's important functions (see Exhibit 3.8) include administering the articles of two of the important international intellectual property treaties, including the Patent Cooperation Treaty and the Paris Convention, both discussed in detail in this chapter.

Patent Cooperation Treaty (PCT)   One of the more important of the treaties administered by the WIPO is the PCT, which provides a unified process by which patents are filed internationally. The PCT was the result of the Washington Diplomatic Conference on Patent Cooperation Treaty

IP Protection	Global Protection System	Classification
• Berne Convention	• Budapest Treaty	• Locarno Agreement
• Brussels Convention	• Hague Agreement	• Nice Agreement
• Film Register Treaty	• Lisbon Agreement	• Strasbourg Agreement
• Madrid Agreement	• Madrid Agreement	• Vienna Agreement
• Nairobi Treaty	• Madrid Protocol	
• Paris Convention	• PCT	
• Patent Law Treaty		
• Phonograms Convention		
• Rome Convention		
• Singapore Treaty on the Law of Trademarks		
• Trademark Law Treaty		
• Washington Treaty		
• WCT		
• WPPT		

E X H I B I T   3 . 8   WIPO Functions

and was signed on June 19, 1970, with 18 contracting states. Since that time, the number of contracting states has grown to 130, with Laos and Honduras scheduled to join in 2006.

Applications filed under the PCT are simply called *international applications* as the applications do not result in a patent (there is no such thing as a PCT patent). The PCT allows applications to be filed in one language, in one place, at which time all contracting states are designated and a singular priority date is created. Upon the filing of a PCT, an international searching authority (ISA) is selected to conduct an international patentability search. After the initial search, the applicant may select a preliminary examining authority to conduct a nonbinding examination to determine patentability.

The PCT advantageously delays the date on which national patent applications must be filed in PCT member countries by up to 30 months from the priority date. The entity filing the international application may elect to see the results of the Preliminary International Examination Report regarding the possible patentability of their application before electing to file in national patenting offices. While the examination of an international application under the PCT may cost several thousand dollars, it is economical versus applying for examination in one or more national authorities.

National Authorities Nearly every country in the world has an agency charged with the protection of intellectual property. Even in the complex digital world in which vast quantities of data are available, it still remains nearly impossible to search every authority that grants patents. However, you could search most of the art published by industrial nations by searching the patents and published applications filed at the following authorities:

Australia
Canada
EPO
France
Japan
Germany
Korea
PCT/WIPO
United Kingdom
United States

Searching Full-Text Major Foreign Patent Documents

Full-text English-language records of foreign patent documents are rarely available. The exceptions are patents granted by the EPO and patents filed by the PCT, which will have English-language titles and claims, and occasionally are written in full-text English. Great Britain, Canadian, and Australian patents are also, of course, published in English.

Generally, searching for the full text of major foreign patent documents can be performed through the databases of individual patenting authorities. Most major patenting authorities such as the United States, United Kingdom, EPO, France, Germany, Japan, Korea, and WIPO provide online access to their databases of patent documents for searching.[21] You should be aware of the ranges of dates that individual foreign patent authority databases cover.

Full-text searches of some collections of foreign documents are also available through a number of Web-based subscription services.[22] These resources are convenient for searching in multiple collections at once, and often include image-searching capabilities as well.

Keywords in Foreign Languages and Simple Translations   The primary challenge presented by full-text searching in foreign patents is constructing useful search queries using foreign language keywords. Be careful when using a two-word concept or phrase for search strings: The word order of the query may need to change during translation. For example, suppose you are conducting a search relating to "aspartic acid" and you need to search for French patent references. In French, the English word *acid* is *acide*, and the word *aspartic* is *aspartique*. However, entering "aspartique acide" as a search string, quotes included, would return a misleading results set, as the phrase would appear in French as "acide aspartique," "l'acide aspartique," or even "d'acide aspartique," depending on how it is used in the sentence.

A good approach to finding whole foreign phrases in their proper form is to query a database of EP or PCT documents with an English search string and to restrict your search to the title, abstract, and claims' fields. If the results list includes documents originally published in the language of interest, you may be able to identify the foreign equivalents of your search string text by skimming the foreign language title and claims. For example, querying esp@cenet with "aspartic acid" would return the reference EP1091929, Secondary Aspartic Acid Amide Esters, which has the French title "Esters D'amides Secondaires D'acide Aspartique."

You may even find a reference that uses a synonym for aspartic acid in French, "acide d'asperge." Compare the two English and French-language claims below, from EP0855915:

- Topical composition according to claim 1 characterized by that it is containing **D-aspartic acid** as amino acid.

- La composition topique selon la revendication 1 caractérisée par qu'elle contient **D-acide d'asperge** comme acide aminé.

Using Machine Translators to Assess Foreign Art   The next obstacle in foreign text searching is interpreting foreign-language results (or hits). Internet translation portals, inaccurate as they can be, are a quick way to discern how relevant a foreign document is to your search. One popular translator is AltaVista's Babelfish translator, at http://babelfish.altavista.com/tr. In order to illustrate the limitations of these tools, compare the AltaVista English translation of the French claim interpreted above:

- La composition topique selon la revendication 1 caractérisée par qu'elle contient **D-acide d'asperge** comme acide aminé.

- The topics composition according to the characterized claim 1 by which it contains D-acid of asparagus like amino acid.

As this example shows, machine translation services may flip some words around and do not necessarily recognize specialized chemical, electrical, mechanical, or computer science–related terms. Nevertheless, they are a convenient way to determine the content of patents that may have been published only once in a language other than English without family members in the U.S., EPO, or PCT systems.

Internet translators are useful for performing simple native language searches, as the following example illustrates:

Hits	Criteria
1398	Full Patent Spec: "Jet d'encre"
	Databases: FRA
	Years: 1836–2006
57	Full Patent Spec: inkjet or (ink adj jet)

As illustrated, a simple native language translation dramatically alters the returned results.

Searching Abstract-Only Databases Another strategy to search non-native language foreign patents is to search abstract-only databases. When performing such a search, you will need to format your query correctly; this is not always the same query you might use when searching full text. When searching abstracts, all proximity modifiers should be converted to Boolean operators, and technologically specific terms should be replaced by broader functional terms whenever possible as abstracts are usually short (100- to 200-word) summaries of the reference.

The following examples show the difference changing a full-text query into a query appropriate for abstract-only searching can have:

The full-text query:

Query	Hits	Criteria
1	8,907	Full Patent Spec: ((radio or rf or infrared or ir or ultrasonic or (wi adj fi) or bluetooth or satellite or laser) *with* (transmit*5 or transmission or send*4 or receiv*3 or reception or signal*4 or messag*3 or data)) *same* (vehicle or car or truck or automobile)
		Databases: JP
		Years: 1836–2006
2	2,198	Full Patent Spec: (((cut or shut or turn) adj off) or cutoff or shutoff or disconnect*3 or break*3) with ((fuel adj (pump or line or inject*3)) or ignition or distributor or spark or plug or wire or batter*3 or power or electric*3 or circuit) and (vehicle or car or truck or automobile)
		Databases: JP
		Years: 1836–2006
	58	Combine query: 1 and 2

Now, if we change the proximity operators to Boolean operators in the first query and use broader functional terms in the second query, we should greatly expand the number of results returned.

Query	Hits	Criteria
3	9,890	Full Patent Spec: ((radio or rf or infrared or ir or ultrasonic or (wi adj fi) or bluetooth or satellite or laser) *and* (transmit*5 or transmission or send*4 or receiv*3 or reception or signal*4 or messag*3 or data)) *and* (vehicle or car or truck or automobile)
		Databases: JP
		Years: 1836–2006

Query	Hits	Criteria
4	100,331	Full Patent Spec: (disabl*5 or imped*4 or block*3 or prevent*4 or inhibit*3 or restrict*3 or stop*4) and (vehicle or car or truck or automobile)
		Databases: JP
		Years: 1836–2006
	2,412	Combine Query: 3 and 4

As illustrated, by simply changing the proximity operators to Boolean terms in the first query and using broader functional terms in the second, the returned results increased from 58 to 2,412.

Value-Added Tools[23]

Derwent World Patent Index (DWPI) Thomson Derwent provides access to over 26.3 million patent documents issued by 42 patenting authorities including the European Patent Office, France, Germany, Japan, the United Kingdom, the United States, and the WIPO.[24] The DWPI is an excellent tool to use when searching global art because each indexed document is given its own new abstract, which is a 200- to 500-word English abstract written by a subject matter expert.

DWPI also provides information on related patent applications that are filed worldwide. However, the biggest benefit of the DWPI is the English language abstract, which greatly improves the searcher's access to non-English-language patent information.

There are many patent search engines you could use to search foreign patents.[25] In many cases, you will find that foreign patent data is searchable only (in English) via the abstracts. Foreign abstract-only searching must be approached differently than similar queries in full-text databases.

Searching Nonpatent Literature (NPL)

It is Sunday morning and you walk down to the end of the driveway to recover a not-so-great throw from the paperboy. As you open to the first page, you begin to peruse the headlines. What happened around the world last night and the day before is documented in-depth for your reading pleasure. When you are finished, you place the newspaper in the recycling bin and continue with your morning routine. If someone were to tell you that the paper contains nonpatent literature, you would probably brush him off as crazy. However, in the world of intellectual property, that specific newspaper could cost you millions of dollars. Dated words of any kind are important to the determination of intellectual property.

The USPTO defines *intellectual property* as creative works or ideas embodied in a form that can be shared or can enable others to recreate, emulate, or manufacture them.[26] You can begin to see the enormous task of searching through the masses of NPL that exist in the world. However, it is not impossible, and with the right tools and knowledge, it can be accomplished with minimal time and effort on the searcher's part.

Nonpatent literature means different things to different people. The sheer knowledge that it is infinite can make any attempt to search seem impossible.

Today, with the arrival of online search engines and the facilitated flow of information, personal Web pages have become a wealth of knowledge, albeit unstructured. NPL is all around us. In terms of protecting intellectual property, the only prerequisite is that it can be dated. Even the date has a caveat, as it is defined as the date when the public gets full access to the information contained in the publication. This can limit NPL greatly, as this date has to be able to be documented.

You might ask what is an invention, and are there boundaries to what can be considered prior art? This is a very good question as current definitions are vague and often interpreted broadly. The prior art is defined by 35 USC § 102, which states: "A person shall be entitled to a patent unless" one of the following occurs. First, an applicant is not entitled to a patent if the invention was "known or used by others in this country (United States), or was patented or described in a printed publication in this or a foreign country" prior to the priority date of the patent. So, as stated, this is obvious: If you are in the United States and "Invention A" existed publicly before "Invention B," then "Invention B" may not receive a patent. If "Invention A" existed publicly outside the borders of the United States but was not documented in a publication or patented by a foreign patent office, then "Invention B" is patentable.

Second, a patent application will be denied if "the invention was patented or described in a printed publication in this (United States) or a foreign country or in public use or on sale in this country, more than one

year prior to the date of the application for patent in the United States."
The added language is very important. When we stated the preceding information, we were not concerned whether the prior art was in existence
before the date of invention. Now we must take into account whether the
prior art existed more than one year before filing of the patent application.
The other important caveat in this statute is that the inventor must file a
patent application within one year of a publication of the said invention;
otherwise, the application can be denied. This rule also makes note of
global publications as prior art; if it is printed it applies, but public use as
previously stated matters only within the borders of the United States.

Finally, a patent applicant is denied a U.S. patent if a patent outside of
the United States was obtained before the date of the patent application in
the United States, and if the application outside the United States was filed
more than 12 months before filing the application in the United States. So,
in order for your own invention not to be used against you, you must file
a U.S. application before a foreign patent is issued and no more then one
year after the filing of that international patent. This rule exists so that an
inventor cannot extend their monopoly on an invention by applying in
different countries over the course of many years in order to extend the 17
to 20 years out indefinitely.

Now that we have defined prior art as it relates to NPL, we will discuss
the search of it. The peceding discussion potentially eliminates a great variety of existing literature but enormous amounts of relevant NPL can still
exist. Where would you access that information? The answers are presented in Chapter 6.

ISSUES PECULIAR TO CERTAIN TECHNICAL DISCIPLINES

Biotechnology

Nearly three decades have passed since the filing of Stanley Cohen and
Herbert Boyer's application for U.S. Patent 4,237,224 entitled "Process for
Producing Biologically Functional Molecular Chimeras." In effect, January
4, 1979, marks the effective date of modern biotechnology's birth. Since
that time, the patent offices around the world have experienced a rapid expansion in the numbers of biotechnology-related applications. The
biotechnological art is complex and requires a skilled searcher, using a

careful approach to constructing text, subclass, and often sequence and chemical structure queries.

Chemical and biotechnology patent searching is not unlike patent searching in the mechanical and electrical arts. The searcher develops keyword and subclass search queries to submit to the various patent databases available. Often, developing comprehensive lists of synonyms can take significant research. Biotechnology synonyms are most often not intuitively apparent. Invention disclosures rarely contain complete lists of synonyms, and the ultimate user may not know all of the possible synonyms for a given molecule or class of molecules.

Chemical and biological entities are referred to in many ways. When approaching chemical names, do so carefully. There are at least two accepted nomenclature systems for organic molecules. IUPAC (International Union of Pure and Applied Chemistry) and CAS (Chemical Abstracts Service, a division of the American Chemical Society) each have separate rules systems governing chemical nomenclature. Known chemical entities are also referred to by one or more common names or even brand names within the patent literature. Most chemical compounds are also registered with CAS. They are then assigned a CAS number (or "registry number"). This number is another way for practitioners and patent writers to refer to a chemical entity. In addition to brands, common names, conventional chemical names, and number codes, biomolecular and chemical entities may have synonyms as a result of how and where they were discovered or developed. Newer compounds are referred to by temporary names that may derive from the name of a company that developed the compound and some number that had significance in the experiments leading to its discovery. This is often observed for compounds under clinical development.

For example, a text search for the active component of the popular smoking cessation drug Zyban will need to include the brand name(s), common name(s), registry numbers, temporary clinical reference names, and chemical names using IUPAC and alternative naming conventions.

Example simple text query for Zyban:

Zyban or wellbutrin or prestwick or Bupropion or Amfebutamon or "31677-93-7" or "34841-36-6" or "HSDB 6988" or "NSC 315851" or "1-(3-chlorophenyl)-2-(tert-butylamino)propan-1-one" or "2-(tert-Buty-lamino)-3'-chloropropiophenone" or "m-Chloro-alpha-tert-butylaminopropionphenone" or "m-Chloro-alpha-tert-butylaminopropiophenone" or "alpha-(tert-Butylamino)-m-chloropropiophenone"

The National Center for Biotechnology Information (NCBI) operates under the auspices of the U.S. National Library of Medicine (NLM). The ability to navigate the NCBI and NLM Web sites and take advantage of the expanding freely available set of features and tools has become requisite for NPL biotechnology searchers. The NLM is the ultimate resource for the National Institutes of Health (NIH), which operates as a part of the U.S. Department of Health & Human Services.

NCBI operates *Entrez*, which is a gateway to the largest source of freely available life sciences information. A search in Entrez will result in publications, sequences, chemical structures, and other information relating to discipline-specific databases, such as markers and mapping data, protein structure and domain data, and even mouse central nervous system gene expression profiles.

You also may search publications that will place a technological development into the public domain. PubMed is useful for that task. Its references and abstracts come from over 4,600 biological, biochemical, and medical journals. PubMed has the original MEDLINE data files and PubMed Central, a digital archive of freely available full-text life sciences journal literature.

Often, journal articles are not freely available; of those, most full-text information can be purchased online, currently by the article, for US$3 to US$20 and through a short-term subscription. Full subscriptions to specific journals are available, but most are also available through a number of large subscription services. Some are expensive, but provide the only way for a searcher to access full-text documents. This is crucial to understand, for an article may be disclosed in a Materials & Methods section, but you may not find it by virtue of the fact that the disclosure may not be apparent in a search of titles, abstracts, and keywords.

The following is a list of organizations that offer publication subscription services. Some specialize in biotechnology, and others are general in scope, having coverage that extends well beyond the chemical sciences. Depending on your level of usage, it may be advisable to obtain subscriptions on an as-needed basis from these publishers:

- Elsevier Science Direct
- Lippincott Williams & Wilkins

- Springer Link
- Oxford University Press

Other sources of NPL can be found in the database files that are accessible through proprietary search engines such as Thomson Dialog or STN by Fiz Karlsruhe. The biotechnology patent searcher often relies on the following databases:

BIOSIS   BIOSIS Previews/RN covers original research reports, reviews, and selected U.S. patents in biological and biomedical areas, with subject coverage ranging from aerospace biology to zoology. Sources for BIOSIS include periodicals, journals, conference proceedings, reviews, reports, patents, and short communications. Bibliographic information, supplementary terms, abstracts, and CAS registry numbers are all searchable.

Producer:	BIOSIS
Coverage:	1969 to date
File size:	8.9 million records
Updates:	Four times per month
File type:	Bibliographic
Content:	Biosciences
Language:	English

BIOTECHABS/BIOTECHDS   Derwent Biotechnology Abstracts covers worldwide literature on all aspects of biotechnology from genetic manipulation through biochemical engineering and fermentation to downstream processing. BIOTECHDS is available only to subscribers. BIOTECHABS is available to nonsubscribers. Sources include journals, patents, and conference contributions. About 30 percent of the database cites patent publications. Patent information, bibliographic information, abstracts, and controlled terms are searchable.

Producer:	Derwent Publications Ltd.
Coverage:	1982 to date
File size:	150,0000 records
Updates:	Every two weeks
File type:	Bibliographic
Content:	Biotechnology
Language:	English

CHEMICAL ABSTRACTS   The Chemical Abstracts (CA) database covers all areas of biochemistry, chemistry, and chemical engineering. CA contains records for documents reported in printed CA from 1967 to the present. Current sources include over 9,000 journals, patents from 26 countries and two international patent organizations, technical reports, books, conference proceedings, and dissertations. Bibliographic terms, indexing terms, and CAS registry numbers are searchable. Over 87 percent of the records also contain CA abstracts, the text of which is searchable. A learning file, LCA, is also available.

Producer:	CAS
Coverage:	1967 to date
File size:	11 million records
Updates:	Biweekly
File type:	Bibliographic
Content:	Biochemistry, chemistry, chemical engineering
Language:	English

CAB ABSTRACTS   The CAB Abstracts (CABA) database covers worldwide literature from all areas of agriculture and related sciences, including biotechnology, forestry, and veterinary medicine. Sources for CABA include journals, books, reports, published theses, conference proceedings, and patents. Bibliographic information, indexing terms, and abstracts are searchable.

Producer:	CAB INTERNATIONAL
Coverage:	1979 to date
File size:	2.1 million records
Updates:	Monthly
File type:	Bibliographic
Content:	Agriculture
Language:	English

Chemical

STN is a multiple-database searching resource collaboratively run by CAS in North America, FIZ-Karlsruhe in Europe, and the Japan Science and Technology Corporation (JST) in Japan. Using STN, it is possible to query the CAS registry file and the DWPI with chemical structure models.

Queries may search for exact structures as well as substructures having additional and/or variable substituent groups. Advanced searchers may also query the MARPAT file, which contains patents that make use of generic or "Markush" structures that can each represent many specifically defined structures related by a common substructure. The chemical structure query capability is excellent for complementing a keyword/subclass search, as it can be used to locate chemical intermediates and compounds that are not referred to by conventional standards. Currently, STN is the only tool available for performing structure queries in these valuable databases. One drawback to STN in general is that it can be expensive, especially for a novice searcher who is unfamiliar with STN pricing structures. Therefore, specific training is highly recommended and is provided periodically at no charge at various localities and online. Structure searches are typically complementary to other search methods and not used as a sole source of references.

Many biological molecules are polymers. DNA and RNA are polymers of nucleic acids, while proteins (or polypeptides) are polymers of amino acids. The sequences of the building blocks of these polymers determine the structures and functions of the molecules they comprise. As such, genetic sequences are of considerable interest to scientists and inventors; they are often the target of a biotechnology patent search. Again, the most comprehensive sequence searches will utilize an STN query tool to directly search the DGENE and sometimes the PCTGEN files. The DGENE file is the most complete source of international patent sequence information. PCTGEN is comprised of PCT (WO) application sequence data and is highly redundant with DGENE. Biological polymers, as unique chemical entities, are submitted to the CAS registry and given a numeric registry number, similarly to other types of molecules, so it is helpful that sequence queries may also be submitted to the registry file using the STN sequence tool. Subsequent cross-referencing of a registry number in the DGENE or DWPI files can find patent documents containing the sequence.

The NCBI provides free Genbank BLAST (Basic Local Alignment Search Tool) searching on its Web site. BLAST is easy to use, though there are some intricacies that can be best understood by attending a periodic free training session. For example, where an academician may wish to mask "common sequences" within a query to avoid frivolous hits, a patent searcher will choose not to mask these "low-complexity regions" because a patent searcher is usually interested in an exact sequence, complexity notwithstanding, rather than evolutionarily related ones. So the patent searcher will uncheck the low-complexity filter where NCBI has it checked by default. One of the various "BLASTable" Genbank databases is known as "pat" (for patent). The pat database contains issued U.S. patent sequences as well as published EP and WO sequences. It does not contain sequences from published U.S. applications, and the coverage for EP and WO is less complete than what is available using STN. For this reason, it is not recommended to rely on NCBI BLAST searches when performing a comprehensive patent search; however, this tool can be very valuable for preliminary searching and when only issued U.S. patents need to be searched. BLAST can also be used to find NPL as well, by querying Genbank's "nr" (non-redundant) database in the same way.

Business Methods

Prior to 1998, no method of doing business was allowed patent protection in the United States. This was known as the business method exception to patentability. However, in 1998, the United States Court of Appeals for the Federal Circuit ruled in *State Street Bank & Trust Co. v. Signature Financial Group* that "since the 1952 Patent Act, business methods have been, and should have been, subject to the same legal requirements for patentability as applied to any other process or method." The ruling in *State Street Bank & Trust Co.* allows for business methods to receive patent protection. An example of a business methods patent is the one-click online payment by Amazon.com (U.S. Patent 5,960,411). The one-click online payment allows Internet users to conveniently make repeated payment on a Web site by clicking only once as opposed to going through multiple processes including user registration, entering credit card number and expiration date, and clicking multiple times during the payment process. Although the Amazon.com business methods patent has been challenged by many, including Barnes and Noble and IPXL, the patent has not been invalidated.

With the rapidly developing technologies in electronic commerce and the Internet, business methods have seen substantial growth in the last 20 years. Furthermore, business methods is an expansive art that involves automated business data processing technologies, including financial data processing, cryptography and computer security, and business management. In searching business methods that cover finance, business, and management, it is advantageous to have more background in finance, business administration, and management than in engineering.

A majority of business method art is located in Class 705 in the USPTO classification system. Class 705 contains only computer-implemented processes related to electronic commerce, the Internet, and data processing involving finance, business practices, management, and cost/price determination. However, other art that can be labeled as "business method type," such as methods of teaching, methods of playing games, and methods of improving crop yields, are classified or cross-classified in other areas according to their technology. Therefore, when searching for a business method, multiple technological areas should be considered and consulted.

When examining patent documents for business methods, do not rely only on figures, drawings, and flowcharts. In many cases, business methods are extensively described within the specification but are not represented in the figures. Furthermore, like mechanical art, business methods involve many generic terms that describe the same step. Careful consideration should be made in formulating text searches, including the use of synonyms.

Of the three major patent authorities (United States, Europe, and Japan), Europe has the strictest requirement for obtaining a business methods patent. Article 52(2) of the EPC states that methods for doing business, mathematical methods, presentations of information, and programs for computers shall not be regarded as inventions. However, many business method applications have been filed and granted at the EPO because the applications have been drafted to meet Article 52(3) of the EPC. Article 52(3) EPC states that although methods for doing business are explicitly excluded from being patented, "a product or a method which is of a technical character may be patentable, even if the claimed subject-matter defines or at least involves a business method." In Japan, a business method is patentable only if the method contains a technical aspect that is real and tangible. Business methods are patentable as long as the methods are implemented by using a computer. Thus, a thorough search of foreign patents and applications is important in performing a complete patent search of business methods.

Because business methods is a rapidly developing field, a search of NPL is also important. In addition to NPL databases such as IP.com, DialogPro, and STN, online search engines like Google and Google Scholar will provide valuable information for the latest developments through news articles, conference papers, thesis papers, company Web sites, and advertisements.

Computer, Software, and Electronics

For the purposes of a patent search, electronics and computer technology can be divided into two categories, each requiring separate search strategies. The first category is hardware, which considers the physical elements and the arrangement of these elements used to accomplish an electronic function. The second category is software, which considers the encoded media (magnetic, optical disk, etc.) used to control the processes performed by the hardware. While computing itself dates back hundreds of years with the development of various mechanical calculators, it was not until the twentieth century that electronics and computer technology began to make a significant impact on the patent world.

Modern electronics hardware dates back at least as far as the development of the transistor in 1948 by John Bardeen and others (U.S. Patent 2,524,035), which replaced the earlier vacuum tube technologies and enabled smaller switching devices, providing multiple advancements in radio, memory storage, and computing technologies. The development of integrated circuitry by Jack Kilby and others (U.S. Patent 3,138,743) in 1959 provided a platform for further miniaturization and an avenue to combine different electronic elements (transistors, diodes, capacitors, etc.) with different functions (amplification, switching, filtering, etc.) on a common substrate.

The developments of electronics hardware have been well documented in the patent literature. In many areas related to electronics and computer hardware the amount of patenting is so large that many overlapping and intersecting patents are found, resulting in a "patent thicket." This patent thicket can be very difficult to navigate, and this section (as well as the next section on electrical engineering patents) will provide some suggestions on how a searcher may organize his search so as to produce the best results in a minimal amount of time.

Modern electronics software dates back at least to the 1930s. A mathematician named Alan Turing, among others, conceived of a theoretical machine that could be programmed to solve any algorithm. While initially existing as a theoretical concept, computational tasks existed requiring the flexibility of such "programmable" machines to perform tasks such as calculating ballistic firing tables for the army during World War II. These initial programmable machines were formed using vacuum tube switches, but eventually transistor and integrated circuit technologies were used as the platform for programmable machines. In the early 1970s, the development of the general-purpose programmable microprocessor by Texas Instruments (U.S. Patent 3,757,306) and others allowed for the variety of computer and computer-controlled devices we enjoy today.

Unlike the case of computer hardware, the literature for computer software has not been well covered by patent documents. In the past, it was believed by many that software patents were unobtainable or unenforceable, and therefore few patents for software-related inventions were filed. In addition, the emergence of open source software, wherein members of a community of programmers contribute pieces to the development of software code, has created a source of prior art that is scattered, poorly indexed, and presents considerable difficulty to the patent searcher.

This section will provide suggestions on how searchers can find the best resources quickly and efficiently to maximize their chances of finding the best prior art for software searches.

Because of the rapid and constant evolution of electrical innovations, there are approaches to searching these patents that are unique. This discussion presents tips for approaching these types of patent searches.

For image searching, computer art is not as drawing intensive as other arts, although drawings are useful for searching. Often, a search in this discipline requires an understanding of abstract concepts whose innovations are nonphysical inventions (e.g., data compression algorithms, routing engines, wireless modulation techniques). When image searching these inventions, the drawings could appear as flow diagrams, state tables, graphs, mathematical formulas, binary strings showing data formats, or even "black box" wiring diagrams (see Exhibit 3.9).

It may be difficult to determine if such a reference is relevant based solely on the drawings. The drawing may disclose an initial concept that is intricately described in the specification but not fully illustrated in the drawing, requiring the patent searcher to read the specification carefully after seeing the drawing. Often, alternate embodiments may be discussed in the detailed description but not shown in the drawings (see Exhibit 3.10).

For computer art, it is often necessary to focus more on classification and text-based searching to find the best prior art. The reason for this is that the inventive concepts involved in computer art are more closely related to

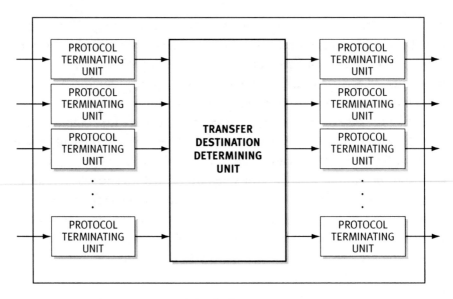

E X H I B I T   3 . 9   **Black Box**

ADDRESS SECTION		DATA SECTION		
MULTI-PATH ID (M)	**TRANSFER PATH NO. (PN)**	**ALLOCATION STREAM COUNT (PC)**	**MAX. STREAM COUNT (PH)**	**MAX. CONTINUOUS ALLOCATION COUNT (PM)**
0	0	2048	2048	1
	1	2048	2048	1
	2	0	0	0
	3	0	0	0
	4	0	0	0
	5	0	0	0
	6	0	0	0
	7	0	0	0
1	0	0	0	0
	1	0	0	0
	2	1365	1365	1
	3	1365	1365	1
	4	1368	1366	1
	5	0	0	0
	6	0	0	0
	7	6	6	0
2	0	0	0	0
	1	0	0	0
	2	0	0	0
	3	0	0	0
	4	0	0	0
	5	1365	1365	1
	6	1365	1365	1
	7	1368	1366	1

E X H I B I T   3 . 1 0   **State Table**

function than to structure. Whereas a mechanical invention may be well defined in terms of the materials, shapes, and arrangement of the parts forming the invention, many computer-related inventions focus on what an invention does (function) rather than what an invention is (structure). Thus, drawings, which are primarily pertinent for showing structure, are less relevant than classification and text-based searching when it comes to many computer and electronics inventions.

Process claims have always been an area of patentability recognized by the U.S. patent system. However, prior to the development of programmable microprocessors, these processes were mostly constrained to steps performed by human intervention to manufacture or use an article or apparatus. The advent of the general-purpose microprocessor removed the necessity of human intervention in many of these process claims and allowed for equivalent structural claims to be provided by including a claim limitation such as "a controller for . . . (insert process steps)," "a processor capable of . . . (insert process steps)," "a computer programmed to . . . (insert process steps)," etc. The more direct applications of these structural claims to software patents have been challenged in the U.S. court system, but precedent such as *State Street Bank & Trust Co. v. Signature Financial Group Inc.* (Fed Cir. 1998) has verified that software can be patented, provided it is more than a mere algorithm and produces a tangible, useful result.

It should be kept in mind by the searcher that search methods used for these computer-related inventions do not apply only to software or computer claims but also to a vast array of devices that use software to achieve the inventive effect. For example, a desktop printer may employ a scanning inkjet print head that ejects tiny drops of ink from a plurality of tiny nozzles during reciprocal scans of the print head so as to form a printed image. An inventor may come along and find that changing the order or timing of the ejection of the ink drops may achieve a useful result such as heat reduction, reduced cross-talk, and so on. In order to achieve this improved result, the inventor may simply reprogram the software used to control the printer to change the order of ink ejection, without changing any structural element of the printer. Thus, while claims to a printer or other concrete device may be presented, the searcher must know whether it is the structure or the function that is at the heart of the invention and frame the search accordingly.

For computer-related inventions, this can be best applied by first determining whether the invention is functional or structural in nature. If the searcher is performing a search based on a set of claims, a clear sign of whether the invention is structural or functional is the presence of limitations such as "a controller for," "control means to," "a memory arranged for," and the like. While these limitations refer to structural components such as memory or control units, it is usually the functions carried out by these components that are the focus of the invention and the searcher should organize his or her search around the problem being solved rather than any structural limitations. If the searcher is performing a search based on a disclosure, the presence of flowcharts explaining the invention will usually be indicative of the invention being functional rather than structural.

Fortunately for the searcher, the U.S. and foreign patent offices have divided many of the patent search classes into both structural and functional areas. If the searcher has determined that the invention is functional, such as in software-based inventions, then, in the case of U.S. patent searching, the area of focus would be one of classes 700 through 707 or 715 through 717, all of which relate to the data processing aspects of computer-related inventions. If the searcher has determined that the invention is structural, such as in application-specific electronic control circuits that involve a specific arrangement or interconnection of elements (shift registers, counters, etc.), classes 326 through 338 may be the best search area. There are also some areas of the U.S. class system such as classes 708 through 714 that were created to address both structural and functional features. Also, when computer software- or hardware-based inventions are used to control a specific device or apparatus, such as an automobile or printer, the best U.S. search area is usually the class associated with the specific device. In the international patent classification system (IPC), section G06 covers computer-related inventions with G06F, G06Q, and G06T applying toward data processing and G06C through G06E and G06D through G06N relating to the computing structures. The IPC and other foreign classification systems have been more reluctant to address computer-related software patents than the United States, especially when concerned with business methods, so foreign searching may be less productive in this area. However, the most recent addition of the international patent classification (IPC8) does include an area for software-based business methods (G06Q). More information on the US and IPC classification systems may be found at www.uspto.gov/web/patents/classification/ and www.wipo.int/classifi cations/en/.

For software searches directed toward generic computer control or busi-ness methods, NPL can be a particularly difficult area to search, but is nec-essary due to gaps in the patent record for software-related inventions. The gaps in the patent record may be partly remedied by reviewing the numerous texts discussing details of the various operating systems and pro-gramming languages available.

Often, bibliographic data obtained from textbooks focusing on general surveys of software development can be the best source for starting a soft-ware search. A searcher dedicated to software searching would be advised to keep an up-to-date library of such general textbooks. Open source soft-ware presents a particularly difficult problem to the searcher because this information is often not well indexed for purposes of searching. Currently, the U.S. patent office is working with those in the open source commu-nity to establish an indexed open source software prior art database, which may result in a better search resource. Currently, IP.com is a resource that allows for submission of defensive disclosures and may be a good source of information in current software developments.

The software used in the operating and programming systems of mod-ern computers, computer networks, and the Internet is evolving at a rapid pace due to diffusion of different ideas and concepts among the various platforms used. This diffusion is driven largely by the Internet, which fa-cilitates communication and cross-pollination of ideas among different pro-grammers fueling rapid development of a multitude of different software solutions to a variety of problems.

An example of this effect is found in the programming language, Ruby, which was originally developed in the 1990s and combines features of many other programming languages, including object-oriented program-ming and common gateway interfacing used in Internet servers. Ruby has been (and is continuing to be) developed by the open source community and is constantly being updated with new features or modified for specific applications by various programmers. Unfortunately, U.S. patent refer-ences are typically published 18 months after filing, and therefore even the newest patents or prepatent publications may be years out of date. There-fore, a searcher would be advised to use the Internet as a primary search tool when searching for rapidly developing software and identify the community involved in a particular area of computer software to find the most current information (for example, http://rubyforge.org/ may be a good source if searching for an invention related to Ruby). Often, there are public forums on such Web sites that can provide valuable information to guide a searcher, or the users and developers within the community may have contact information on the Web site, and a carefully phrased inquiry to one of these users (keeping confidentiality in mind) may provide fruitful results.

The computer industry is fond of acronyms. It is not uncommon to see a sentence such as "You should bit error rate and time domain reflectometry test that integrated service digital network for far end cross-talk on the unshielded twisted pair category 6" written as "You should BERT and TDR that ISDN for FEXT on the UTP CAT6." If the searcher is looking for a concept that is expressible in acronym form, both the acronym and the full expression should be used in a text search inquiry (i.e., ISDN or "integrated service digital network") in order to assure that relevant prior art documents are not overlooked simply because the prior art document does or does not use an acronym.

Computer-related inventions have many terms that are used interchangeably, even when the inventions are technically different. For example, the terms *packet*, *cell*, *frame*, *datagram*, and *envelope* have been used interchangeably. This presents particular difficulties when key terms are domain specific, meaning that the analyst cannot consult a general thesaurus to locate synonyms for the telecommunications version of the term *packet*. Awareness of newer terminology that may be used in place of older terms as a technology evolves is necessary.

The best way to enhance awareness of alternative terminologies for a common technology is the use of forward and backward citation of a related patent. For example, if a searcher were looking for an invention related to flashlights, he or she might think that *flashlight* or *flash-light* would be a universally art accepted term and limit a text search accordingly. Use of this term creates a bias in the text search results toward references that use the term *flashlight* and few references will be produced using an alternative term. However, performing a backward citation search or a forward citation search on one of the references produced may result in other patents that use other terms such as *penlight* or *torch* to describe a flashlight. These terms may then be added to future text search inquiries to obtain a fuller, more accurate depiction of the relevant art terminology.

There are some databases of particular interest in the computer, software, and electronic arts. Because computer technology develops rapidly, patent searchers should consult multiple NPL sources.

The following is a sample of prominent databases that are useful for computer technology and that contain millions of text searchable records.

- IEEExplore
- Association for Computing Machinery (ACM)
- Softbase
- Ei Compendex
- INSPEC
- National Technical Information Service (NTIS)
- Japanese Science & Technology (JICST-EPlus)
- PASCAL

The history of electrical engineering (EE) goes back to the early nineteenth century, when basic direct current (DC) motors and generators were constructed and the basic theories of electricity and magnetism were developed by scientists such as Faraday, Maxwell, and others. However, it was not until the twentieth century that patent activity in EE became dominant.

The development of alternating current (AC) power generation, transmission, and distribution and the invention of new devices to use transmitted power such as the electric light, radio, television, and so on, resulted in a flood of patent applications in the EE field. Combined with the computational and programmable abilities of microprocessors in the last few decades, as well as the emergence of a variety of sensor technologies, EE has experienced an explosive growth, which has been mirrored by the rapid increase in patent filings over the past several years. This growth has resulted in a series of overlapping patents within the EE field, which has often been referred to as a "patent thicket." This may present a problem to the patent searcher because, in contrast to the case of software patents in which there is not enough patent literature, for EE-related patents there is an overabundance of patent literature that can be very difficult to sort through.

This section will provide suggestions to help the searcher navigate through these "packet thickets."

While classification and text-based searching are both useful techniques applicable to EE patent searching, a stronger and more efficient technique in many cases would be backward and forward citation searching.

The main defect with classification searching in EE arts is that individual patent subclasses in the EE area often contain hundreds or thousands of individual patents. Numerous subclasses may need to be searched, resulting in an extremely time-consuming task consisting of the analysis of thousands of patents. Even if a searcher took the time to go through each of the patents, there is a good probability that he or she would miss a highly relevant reference based on the fatigue generated when spending so much time on a search. Also due to the crowded nature of many EE technologies, many specialized patent subclasses with very complex definitions have been created by the U.S. and foreign patent offices. Since developments in EE technology often occur more frequently than the refinement of the definitions for these subclasses, patents often get misplaced, and thus even a comprehensive search of a patent subclass dedicated to the target invention may overlook a pertinent patent.

The main defect with text searching in the EE arts is that the terminology chosen for the text search may be out of date or incomplete. Even the most studious researcher in a particular technology can often be surprised at the way some inventors may use different terminologies for a common element. Many different corporations and independent inventors may be involved in a specific technical field, each describing their technology in a slightly different way. For example, inkjet print heads used in digital printers may be referred to as *printheads* by Xerox, *recording heads* by Canon, and *pens* by Hewlett-Packard, while all refer to an identical element.

In contrast to the preceding methods, backward and forward citation searching take advantage of the "patent thicket" and turn this thicket from a disadvantage to an advantage. In contrast to a "thicket," an intelligent searcher may look at a crowded patent collection as an interwoven fabric of intersecting patents. Pulling upon the correct thread of this fabric may untangle the "thicket" and quickly lead to useful results in a patent search. Backward searching may most successfully be applied to patents discovered to have claimed a common element to the target invention. The reason for this is that patent examiners base their search almost exclusively on what is being claimed and the references that they cite are likely to possess these claimed features. Forward citation searching may most successfully be applied to patents having disclosed features or embodiments unique to the patent, regardless of whether these features are claimed. The reason for this is that patent examiners will often cite base or early patents disclosing a unique feature in later patents attempting to improve upon this feature. A repeated iteration of backward and forward citation searching, combined with appropriate selection among the results of such searching for subsequent backward and forward citation searching, is a valuable strategy to cull the best results quickly for a crowded art area. The following are tips for searching in EE technology.

While backward and forward citation searching are suggested as an optimizing technique, it is important to first identify patents to use as a starting point for such citation searching. A quick way to accomplish this is with a text search focusing on the title, abstract, or claim fields of patents. Many of the commonly used online search engines such as those found at www.micropatent.com allow you to choose whether to search the whole specification or just portions of the specification such as the abstract. Often, performing a text search on a whole specification produces many irrelevant references that refer to the particular search term as an alternative or without any key importance. However, references that refer to the desired search terms in the abstract, title, or claims are more likely to be centrally relevant to what the searcher is looking for.

As previously explained, while classification searching is not as productive as an iterative citation search strategy for crowded arts, it is often useful to find the general areas where the most relevant patents are classified. If citation searching fails to produce desired results and sufficient search time is allowed, resorting to classification searching may be a necessary step to ensure an exhaustive search. Often, the correct classification of a target invention that is being searched for is very difficult to identify using only the definitions from U.S. or IPC patent classification definition, especially in a crowded, quickly evolving art where patent subclass definitions may quickly lose their relevancy. A better way to identify the best classification search areas would be to simply note the classification of the most pertinent patents produced based on initial text searching of abstracts, titles, and claims.

More information on the U.S. and IPC classification systems may be found at www.uspto.gov/web/patents/classification/ and www.wipo.int/classifications/en/.

The best starting patents for backward citation searching are usually ones that claim a feature that is the target of the search. The reason for this is that the patent examiner who issued the patent had to previously search for these features and was likely to cite a reference or references including similar features. Thus, even if a searcher were to find a patent with a date after a critical date, if this patent claimed features in common with the target invention, then this patent could still prove useful as a source for backward citation. The best starting patents for forward citation searching are ones with a basic primary embodiment dealing with a feature that is the target of the search. Usually, these patents are frequently cited in future patents dealing with improvements of the basic primary embodiment.

Once a good starting set of patents is established, expansion of the search space may be accomplished by appropriate forward and backward citation searching. Selection of the best results from this citation search may serve as a basis for a subsequent citation search. Repeated iteration of this technique can often quickly isolate the most pertinent patents to the target invention. In much the same way that there are seven degrees of separation between any two people, it may be argued that any two patents within a common technical discipline may be connected by a limited number of iterative citations.

For crowded technical arts, such as EE, NPL should be only a secondary source, whereas the patent literature should be the primary focus of the search.

Typically, the driving force behind scientific and technical (nonpatent) literature is exploration of basic science as determined by grant endowments or potential for future innovation. For many of the EE innovation areas, the technology is far beyond the basic science stage and the driving force behind the patent literature is potential for commercialization. This results in most of the technical details, which are often the focus of new inventions, being primarily found within the patent literature for EE-related inventions. However, there are some exceptions, such as in the use of new materials within conventional EE structures that may warrant nonpatent or specialized searching as discussed in the next section.

There are some cases in which emergent EE technologies are not particularly crowded and involve recently developed materials or structures presenting a particular challenge to the searcher. While the citation strategies previously discussed may still be useful in these cases, other techniques must often be employed to ensure a successful and comprehensive search. Searching in these areas may not only be productive for searchers looking for a particular target invention, but for inventors who desire to fully exploit the potential of these new materials structures and understand the development of emerging technologies at the early stages. Two particular areas, micro electromechanical systems (MEMS) and nanotechnology, present particular interest as having cross-disciplinary applications over a wide range of EE-related areas such as sensors, optical relays, memory architectures, and the like.

MEMS emerged in the 1980s as refinements in integrated circuit manufacturing allowed for the creation of three-dimensional structures of a size in the micrometer range. Such structures were designed to be capable of controlled bending based on an electrical input or capable of producing an electrical output based on external effects such as motion, temperature, radiation, or pressure. Presently, such devices are used in a variety of applications, including sensors (motion, chemical, etc.), as ink ejection elements in printers, as radio frequency switches, in biological processing devices, and with reflective elements to produce displays or fiber-optic switching devices.

Nanotechnology employs the use of crystalline material with a granularity of less than 100 nanometers, or molecular structures with particular geometric shapes, to achieve novel material properties. Based on quantum or chemical effects, these materials provide enhanced mechanical, electrical, optical, magnetic, or other properties. Combined with more conventional EE structures and elements, these materials are currently producing a variety of new types of memory systems, flat-panel displays, and chemical/biological sensors.

While still limited in scope, there are a few resources in the U.S. and IPC classification systems for dealing with MEMS and nanotechnology inventions. In the IPC classification system, section B81B is devoted to microstructural devices and systems, while B81C is devoted to the manufacture of such systems. In the U.S. classification system, class 438 typically deals with the fabrication processes of MEMS devices. The U.S. classification has recently developed a new class (977) exclusive to nanotechnology, and the IPC has a similar (but more limited) section (B82B) for this field.

More information on the U.S. and IPC classification systems may be found at www.uspto.gov/web/patents/classification/ and www.wipo.int/classifications/en/.

When dealing with technologies employing fundamentally new materials or structures, rather than different combinations of older materials or structures to create a new effect, it is useful to track the key inventors or assignees (owners) of the patents to identify the most pertinent references. Often, a single inventor or assignee will possess most of the basic teachings at the early stages, and identification of one patent in this group can quickly lead to a comprehensive understanding of the technology's development. For example, an early player in nanotube-based memory devices is a company called Nantero. A simple search of "Nantero" within the assignee field of an appropriate patent search engine produces all 19 of their current patents (at the time of writing). By examining the references cited in these patents, the searcher can quickly gain an understanding of the development and state of the art of this technology by Nantero and others. The searcher should be warned that this technique must sometimes be modified when applied to larger companies involved in emerging technologies, such as Hewlett-Packard and Canon. Since such companies have very large patent portfolios, simple assignee searches are inefficient and additional modifiers should be used (inventors, keywords, etc.) to focus the search.

Often, patents granted for applications in emerging technologies such as MEMS and nanotechnology will have numerous citations to NPL. The patents granted in these fields are often broad in scope, and the inventors and attorneys filing the application want to make sure that any relevant reference is considered by the patent examiner. This leads to numerous citations to supporting scientific and technical papers involving the conceptual and experimental background behind the patent application. Therefore, the search of patent databases can also lead to pertinent NPL for an intelligent patent searcher who studies the cited references.

Of course, in emerging technologies, sources other than patents must be more carefully considered. Often, due to the numerous different published scientific journals, it can be very difficult for the searcher to identify and sort the best references. In this case, the bibliography of general textbooks often can provide the searcher with the best source of indexed citations concerning an emergent art. A searcher dedicated to searching in fields involving an emergent technology is advised to maintain a current library of textbooks in the targeted field.

Mechanical Engineering

Patent figures are instrumental in quickly determining the focus, important features, and structural interrelations of inventions in the mechanical arts. Consider a simple invention such as a stapler. When using a particular stapler, instead of putting the papers to be stapled directly under the very end of the device, a user slides the paper further between the base and stapling section. The stapler has a leverage mechanism jutting from the end opposite the hinge that allows a user to put more force upon the pages so as to be able to staple more pages together. It is easier to view the drawings than to read a description of its structures and how to use it. Usually, the pictures offer as much information that will be needed for a mechanical search as text searching. The following are guidelines that can be used in a mechanical prior art search:

- *View all drawings of pertinent references.* It is important to keep in mind that the cover page drawing may not be the most exemplary drawing. If a reference appears to have any remote relevance, all figures should be viewed. If you find a figure that catches your eye, you should find the text in the specification that describes any features associated with the figure. Further, a particular reference may show features of interest in drawings and not even discuss them. The focus of the reference may be on something entirely different.

- *The specification in the patent you are reviewing may not help you.* Because mechanical patent documents are replete with generic terminology, phrases, and synonyms that are difficult to text search, just reading the specification may not help show the interrelations of mechanical components.

- *Choose your search engine carefully.* Because it is critical to view all of the drawings, you should use a search engine that provides this capability.

Mechanical patent documents contain fewer naming conventions than other technical disciplines and therefore contain numerous ways of describing the same thing. Synonyms used to describe components of a device can be misleading.

In the mechanical arts, old patent documents often contain hidden information that provide excellent teachings of simple mechanical devices. For example, U.S. 550,334 provides a conventional design for a sprocket mechanism for a bicycle from 1895. The patent particularly deals with the design of the sprocket wheel and how the spokes sit within the sprocket. A newer mechanical patent may breeze over a particular subsystem because it is well known. U.S. 2006/0061207, which discloses a sprocket system, glosses over the more conventional aspects of the sprocket, such as the spokes, which are provided for in the prior art. This invention instead focuses on the connections that mount the sprocket, as well as the materials and manufacturing methods used for making the sprocket. While sprocket design has undergone a degree of evolution over the years, spoke design has less "wiggle room" for novelty. The details of that subsystem may be found in a very old patent document that focuses exclusively on that concept. If you were focusing on the spoke subsystem of a sprocket assembly, you may have to look at the earlier art where there was greater flexibility for this subsystem. Additionally, a particular technology may have come and gone over the years and been forgotten, but it is possible that someone will accidentally reinvent it.

ESTIMATING SEARCH TIME

So how long does it take to complete a search and know that it is both comprehensive and thorough? The answer differs for every search, and it is a dilemma. It may not matter to an in-house searcher who has been given sufficient time and opportunity to complete the request. Otherwise, conduct a quick overview of general keywords and use the information to give the amount of time it will take to sort through these patents and to write up a report. The analyst can then at the conclusion of his search recommend the additional searching in certain areas that the analyst did not have time to cover. In this way, you will conduct the best possible search in a cost-effective and timely manner.

NOTES

1. *Merriam-Webster's Collegiate Dictionary*, 11th ed.
2. See 35 USC § 112.
3. See 35 USC § 101; 35 USC § 112.
4. See 35 USC § 102 and 35 USC § 103 for the definitions of U.S. novelty and obviousness.
5. For example, the phrase "*Four rectangular uprights supporting a planar surface*" describes a *table!* (www.lib.utexas.edu/engin/patent-tutorial/tutorial/patenttutorialframeset.htm)
6. This fact is supported by recent Federal Circuit case law.
7. This is just an example to alert the reader to the complexity of patent law. Teaching patent law is neither the purpose nor the scope of this book.
8. Any comments, advice, or opinions from the non-attorney searcher should relate to the technology in question and not the law.
9. Similar hierarchical criteria and methods for marking a potentially relevant reference and final determination of (the degree of) relevancy of marked documents discussed earlier should be applied here, too.
10. USPTO, Class Definitions Manual.
11. See definitions for US Class 375, subclasses.
12. Hierarchical criteria and methods for marking a potentially relevant reference and final determination of (the degree of) relevancy of marked documents discussed earlier should be applied here, too.
13. In the United States, the patent applicant submits patent and nonpatent literature for USPTO consideration in an Information Disclosure Statement (IDS) filed with a Form 1449. The patent examiner cites prior art on a Form 892. If a patent reference was applied by the examiner during prosecution, it will be discussed in an office action. The office action can be found in the patent file history. Landon IP, Inc. sells electronic and paper copies of USPTO patent file histories.
14. Taiwan is the only notable absentee among industrial nations.
15. The conference was called "Munich Diplomatic Conference in Setting up a European System of Grant of Patents" and is also referred to as the "Munich Convention."
16. This is different than the European Patent Office, which is the main organ of the European Patent Organization.
17. Turkey, Bulgaria, and Romania are currently being considered for EU membership.
18. Main office in Munich, branches located in The Hague and Berlin.
19. Convention Establishing the World Intellectual Property Organization, Article 3.
20. See www.wipo.int/members/en/ for a complete list of members.
21. See portal at www.uspto.gov/web/menu/other.html for other major foreign patent authorities.
22. See Chapter 6.
23. A Value Added Tool is a tool that adds material or index information to references in which it indexes.
24. These 42 authorities are covered: Argentina, Australia, Austria, Belgium, Brazil, Canada, China, Czechoslovakia, Czech Republic, Denmark, European Patent Office, Finland, France, Germany, Germany (East), Hungary, India, Ireland, Israel, Italy, Japan, Luxembourg, Mexico, Netherlands, New Zealand, Norway, PCT, Philippines, Portugal, Romania, Russian Federation, Singapore, Slovakia, South Africa, South Korea, Soviet Union, Spain, Sweden, Switzerland, Taiwan, United Kingdom, United States of America. Patent-related items from *International Technology Disclosures* (ceased publication June 1994) are also included.
25. See Chapter 6 for databases and their coverage.
26. www.uspto.gov/main/glossary.

CHAPTER 4

Patent Analysis

This chapter briefly presents the differences between a prior art search and patent analysis. It also provides specific guidance on how to communicate the findings of patent analysis in a formal report. There is more to complex patent analysis than is covered in the chapter, so this text is meant to provide merely an overview for the patent searcher.

THE PRECURSOR TO PATENT ANALYSIS

By some estimates there are as many as 40 million patent documents available electronically. Whatever the actual number, clearly there is a significant amount of structured patent data that can be searched efficiently. The industry evolved from limited indexing and abstracts in 1980 to millions of full-text documents in 2007.

The continued explosion in the availability of patent data will allow the quality of patent searches to improve dramatically. More importantly, vast resources of retrievable patent data will transform the competitive intelligence function at companies and consulting firms worldwide. You can observe the trends in data accessibility by tracing the content of articles published in the exceptional industry journal *World Patent Information*, even over the past few years.

Patents are no longer monitored by only the legal community. Many business, product, and research managers at major companies monitor and analyze patent information for strategic business purposes. Universities have teams of technology managers devoted full time to "technology transfer" doing the same. Companies hire analysts, consultants, and licensing experts to help them with research and development strategies, patent portfolio valuations, and technical intelligence. A casual observer cannot read about intellectual property (IP) without noticing all the talk about patent valuations, auctions, indexes, trolls, "Rembrandts in the Attic"—you name it. You will observe many more of these developments in the future. The patent consulting industry is here to stay.

Patent information represents the largest source of technical information in the world. As most of it becomes easily accessible, analysts will search it, compare it, and synthesize it. Therefore, this chapter will provide you with an introduction to patent analysis. (By the way, the sexy term for patent analysis is *patent analytics*, but we will use the term *analysis* because it does not require a definition. Everyone knows what *analysis* means).

Searches versus Analyses: What's the Difference?

You may be thinking "What's the difference between a patent search and a patent analysis? Aren't they the same thing?" The answer is "no." The prior art search is an attempt to find evidence of patents and technical publications in order for an attorney to assess patentability, novelty, clearance, infringement, or state of the art. Its purpose is to find technologically relevant material to address a specific legal need.

Patent analysis is based on the same type of searching, where the analyst will rely on the same types of databases and conduct searches in the same techniques of the prior art search. However, patent analysis extends the patent search to a technological assessment that addresses a business or research need.

Often, product managers, business managers, research and development (R&D) teams, or IP strategists will conduct or commission patent analyses. With the exception of a patent map, the defining feature of patent analysis is an assessment that is derived by comparing across patent data and not of the patent itself.

In order clarify the difference, the following table compares patent searches to patent analyses.

	Patent Searches	**Patent Analyses**
Audience	Attorneys and agents	Business managers, research managers, product managers, IP strategists
Assessment Type	Minimal. Provides evidence of prior art to an attorney or agent	Technological
Purpose	Assist with legal opinion; assist with patent prosecution or litigation	Solve a business or research problem; assist with licensing initiative or marketing preparation; determine research cooperation
Scope	May be broad and deep, but usually results in a legal assessment of individual or groups of patent documents	Broad and deep and usually a technology assessment across patents
Size	Small to large studies	Usually large studies
Data Handling	Assessment of the legal impacts of the data is important	Synthesis and visualization of the data is important
Tools Used	Sometimes conducted with the assistance of sophisticated software tools	Often requires the assistance of sophisticated software tools
When Conducted	Anytime before or during patent prosecution or after patent grant	Usually precedes the legal function and is conducted during the R&D or product management stage
Risk Type	High legal and business risks	High business risks
Customization	Moderately customized	Highly customized
Related Use	Answer specific legal questions or problems	Sometimes part of a larger study, such as a competitive intelligence or market research initiative

FEATURES OF PATENT ANALYSES AND REPORTING

Now that we have established that patent searches and analyses have different characteristics but are based on the same mechanics of searching, we will now discuss the subtleties of analysis. Though some of the principles that follow could apply to a legal search, they are intended here to define the requirements of business-related patent analysis.

Establish Clear Objectives

The classic response from people who receive patent analysis reports is, "Very nice, now what do I do with it?" Why does this response happen? Usually, it happens because those doing the analysis do not really understand the objective of the person who requested the analysis. So prior to any patent analysis, the searcher and search recipient must agree on the objective for doing the analysis.

How do you know what the objective is? First, you ask. Then, like a skilled salesperson, you go a level deeper. You ask about the objective behind that stated objective, or perhaps even the objective behind that, until you understand, for example, that your customer does not just want you to make a patent landscape assessment, but that he wants you to make a patent landscape because his customer is exploring an acquisition of Acme Inc. and wants to know if its patents have value. You will better tailor your searching and analysis when you know the objectives of the study.

The Importance of the Data

Even when the analyst and the customer (recipient) understand the real objective for the analysis, some analyses miss the mark. Why does this happen? The culprit tends to be "bad data." Many patent analysis organizations build their practices around specific automated tools or algorithms, and make the quality or experience of the analyst a secondary consideration. The tools themselves may be good tools when used by a skilled analyst, but they are a poor substitute for the mind of the analyst. Put another way, in analogy, though you should expect the winner of the Daytona 500 to have a certain quality and standards of tools (the fast car) to even be in the race, you are better off betting on the driver in conjunction with the car.

Likewise, in patent analysis, the customer should bet on the patent analyst and his ability to use the correct tools, even if that means his brain and a simple spreadsheet program. More important than software tools, the analyst's analytical skills and judgment are paramount.

As the analyst, you should know your subject matter in detail. You should seek to understand the technology, the analysis process, and the objectives of your customer. You should use only the set of analytical tools required to meet the objectives of your customer. Two imperatives in this role are access to reliable patent databases, both commercial and public, and access to a spreadsheet or database management software program to manipulate and present data.

A comprehensive patent database and method for displaying your results will provide 80 percent or more of your analysis tool needs. There are many data analyses and visualization tools that are available to you. Some of them may be useful, but nothing provides as much value ("bang for the buck") as a spreadsheet program.

Search Technology built a software program called Vantage Point that is an excellent visualization tool. In fact, as of the writing of this book, even Derwent Analytics was based on Vantage Point technology.

A myriad of other software programs, such as Microsoft Visio or Mindjet Mindmap, can assist you with visualization and reporting. However, no software tools will substitute for actually reading patents, and in a typical analysis, there will be many patent documents to consider.

The Trouble with Shortcuts

What if you do not have time to read through a lot of patents yourself? You hire someone else to do it for you, and in fact, some companies have teams of internal patent analysts who conduct complex patent studies on a full time basis. Technical shortcuts fall short because the very nature of patents requires technologists to base assumptions drawn from patents on minimally correlative data. The result is equivalent to basing who will win a sports championship on who pays the highest player salaries. It matters, but not that much.

The worst culprit of the minimally correlative data bunch is patent citations analysis. The patent that receives a comparatively large number of examiner citations often describes an important technology in its field, but sometimes it means nothing. Also, since the first examiner citations will not appear in the public record until three years after the first filing of a patent application, the data signal is old. Despite the limitations of citation searching for patent analysis, it is a useful tool for prior art searching as discussed in Chapter 3.

Capturing the Data Set

Once you understand your analysis, determine how you will begin. Your first task is to capture the data you intend to analyze. You accomplish this by structuring a search to a data set large enough to include all the documents you want to analyze. Then you sort through that dataset to separate, identify, and categorize the relevant results. This process can prove daunting for large datasets, and is yet another reason to clearly define the objective.

Many analysts take shortcuts when acquiring data by trying to design searches to capture just the desired data and leave behind everything else. This may work when one is trying to find needles in a haystack, as you would in a prior art search, but it fails when one is trying to analyze needles in the haystack where types of needles have gradients of relevance. A good heuristic when you do not have a tightly defined technology, like a specific molecule or DNA sequence, is if your search has a density of more than one good record in every four, then you have missed something important in your search. You likely will base your analysis on bad data. Conversely, if you conduct a search and do not sort data at all—and this happens in more reports than you might expect, particularly when the analysis tools take precedence over the quality of the analysts knowledge in the technical field—then your analysis will certainly be based on bad data.

For example, consider C-60 molecules, known as Buckyballs or Buckminster Fullerenes. These are essentially soccer ball–shaped balls of carbon. How might you inadvertently produce a bad data set during a patent analysis? First, if you just search (Buckyballs or Buckminster Fullerenes), then you will capture the majority of Buckyball patents, but you will not capture the first Buckyball patents that inventors filed before people called the molecules "Buckyballs" or "Buckminster Fullerenes."

If you searched (C-60 and (Buckyballs or Buckminster Fullerenes), then you would still have the same problem. If you searched (C-60 or (Buckyballs or Buckminster Fullerenes), then you capture those first Buckyball patents, plus all the C-60 patents that are not shaped like a ball. Add (C-60 or (Buckyballs or Buckminster Fullerenes)) and ball, and you generate a better results set, but you still miss important patent records. What if the patent drafter used "spherical," for example? Furthermore, not all Bucky-balls are C-60. Some are C-120, C-180, etc. Are these relevant? It depends on the customer's objective.

Underlying most objectives is a requirement for a freedom-to-operate search focus or a requirement for a patent landscape search focus. What this means for your analysis in the Buckyball example is that if you have a free-dom-to-practice focus around a C-60 Buckyball invention, then you may not need to worry about the C-120s or the C-180s, but you better not miss any C-60s through too narrow a search.

If your analysis is for a patent landscape, capturing most, if not all, the C-60 Buckyball patents may prove good enough for your customer's pur-poses, but you do not want to miss any C-120s or C-180s that offer a better solution than the C-60 your customer has chosen to explore. This bottom line is to cast a wide net and take the time to sort the good from the bad.

Processing the Results

All reports consist of text, charts, graphs, and tables. All these elements need to have a purpose. A third reason patent analyses fail, even when the analyst has captured good data, rests with how the analyst processes that data. Text, charts, graphs, and tables must support the recipient's objective.

The most frequent abuse on a patent analysis report is to include an un-qualified patent count. Just because a company has more patents than an-other company does not mean it has a lead over that other company. What is the focus of those inventions in the count? What is their quality? How new or old are they? Are the inventors still working in the field? Are the inventors still with the company? In short, go ahead and count, but qual-ify the results.

The first qualification, always, involves categorizing results so that all quantitative measures represent apples to apples, not apples to oranges comparisons. Subcategorize to make the results even clearer, so red apples are measured against red apples, and green against green.

The second qualification is to personalize the results. A given company does not invent—inventors within that company invent. Inventors tend to follow a line of research and tend to have a direction for that research. If you find something interesting during a patent analysis, know who invented the technology the patent document describes. Analyze some of his or her other work. A single patent is like a single chapter in a book. The whole body of an inventor's work tells a more complete story.

With many studies, the body of work by an inventor tends to matter. Often, it allows you to gauge the direction of his research and development efforts. For example, if an inventor's important catalyst patent focuses on how to produce a synthesized product cheaply, then all you know is the focus of that patent. If all the patents of that inventor also focus on producing a synthesized product cheaply, than you can project that his or her present or future work will have this focus and take action accordingly. What if the inventor's focus on all other patents was catalysts for synthesizing better products, not cheaper products? Might that affect how his or her company will react to an infringement or a request for a license?

Displaying Results

A number of books describe how to produce excellent charts, graphs, and tables. *The Visual Display of Quantitative Information* by Edward Tufte (Graphics Press, 1986) is a good source. In all cases, follow conventional wisdom when displaying analyses. Label all charts and their axes. Ensure that all the data points are clearly visible. Clearly communicate values on axes and data points. Label the data points. If the data points are not clear, redesign the chart or recut the data. Also, do not depend on color as a differentiator if your customer might print or copy the report. The world still has more black-and-white printers and copiers than color counterparts. (If you let Microsoft Excel automatically select the colors on your charts, they will tend to do well with black-and-white printers.)

Functional charts and graphs trump form as far as producing a report that delivers on your customer's objective. First, make charts, graphs, and tables work. Then consider how to make them look better. You will soon discover that the charts, graphs, and tables that work the best also tend to look better than those that do not work. Form tends to follow function, just so long as you start with function first.

Also, include within your charts, graphs, and tables the four most basic tenants of strategy: time, space, material, and risk. Time tells customers what period you investigated when you produced the results. Space tells recipients what authorities and types of data you used in the investigation. Material tells customers what is actually in the investigation. Risk tells customers what databases you used so he or she can assess the probability that important data points were not within the pool of data you researched.

(Try this sometime: Put the same underlying search string in competing databases. You will get different results in almost all cases. That is why an expert analyst will not depend on just one database for a comprehensive report.)

Sample Patent Analysis Report

In order to apply some of these principles, it is useful to have a basic example. The very simple patent landscape study that follows relates to golf club heads, a technology that is easy to communicate and understand. The writing in **bold italics** that follows provides direction on how to report the results of an analytical search.

Golf Club Head Patent Landscape Study

(Sample)

Start with the purpose for the analysis, which should include your customer or search recipient's objective. Place the purpose early in the report so that the reader will know specifically what the analysis is for, and also, what it is not for.

Purpose of this Document

The purpose of this document is to serve as a sample patent landscape study for review by prospective decision makers. It is general in nature and intended to provide readers with the type of information a patent landscape study will deliver. It includes common analysis techniques familiar to most professionals.

Usually, the next section is an executive summary. Here, you inform the audience of what follows in the rest of the report. One page is usually sufficient to communicate the major points.

Summary of Golf Club Head Inventions 2001–2005

All companies involved in golf club head research participate in a type of performance "arms race" in which the goal is to give every possible advantage to players, within PGA standards, that could help those players to improve their game. Inventions revolve around making a golf ball consistently travel truer and farther for both novices and experienced players. Upon investigating golf club patents, inventions to do the following proved the most common:

- Efficiently transfer energy from the club head to the ball with a minimum of energy lost due to vibration or unfavorable club or ball compressions . . .

- Optimally distribute weight in the club head to create a preferred, typically lower, center of gravity in the club without harming the durability of the club . . .

The main body of your report includes a detailed discussion and often charts, graphs, tables, and commentary. A Pareto chart (also known as 80/20 analysis) like the one in Exhibit 4.1 is a good place to begin as it puts quantitative informa-

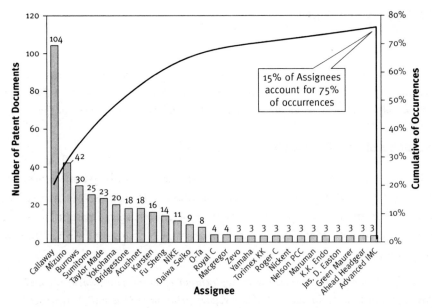

E X H I B I T   4 . I   **Assignee Identification**

tion into clear perspective. Since charts, graphs, and tables tend to favor quantitative analyses, the corresponding text allows you to communicate the qualitative aspects of the data set.

Discussion of the Analysis and Results

Callaway Golf is a clear leader in patenting, followed by several American and Japanese companies. Nineteen percent of assignees account for 75 percent of occurrences; a number that is in agreement with a Pareto Analysis: 20 percent of the members in a set tend to account for 80 percent of the results.

Although Callaway Golf has more than twice the number of patents displayed by its nearest rival, the overall slope of patent documents to assignees on the Pareto chart above is characteristic of a distribution . . .

You can include your perspectives on time and trend as in the patent trend below. In other words, you have investigated the past and present so that you and others can better predict the future (see Exhibit 4.2).

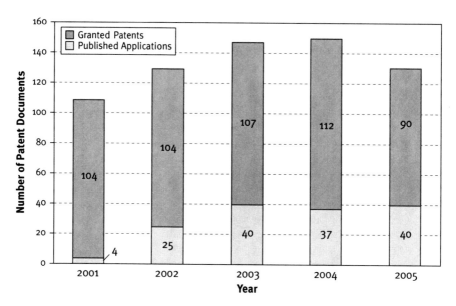

E X H I B I T   4 . 2   **Total Patent Documents Over the Past Five Years**

Patenting Trends

Modest increases in patent activity appear on a year-to-year basis regarding the total number of patent documents published from 2001 to 2005. This may be accounted for by developments in the technology; however, it is worth noting that the U.S. Patent and Trademark Office (USPTO) has granted fewer patents in the past few years due to their overwhelming backlog of unexamined patent applications. In other words, there may have been even more patent activity (more pending patent applications) that is not evident from this chart. Based on our analysis of nonpatent publications, the growth trend in golf club head design is expected to continue as companies seek to offer even the slightest edge . . .

Include some aspect of where patent activity occurs so your customer can see leading centers of activity (see Exhibit 4.3).

Leading Countries

The United States appears to dominate the total number of patent documents pertaining to golf club heads. Further investigation shows that a substantial portion of the U.S. patent documents belong to entities having fewer than three patents . . .

When you have familiarity with a topic and know or discover something of interest, include it. Using a different example from the golf study

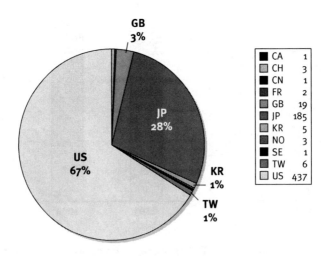

CA	1
CH	3
CN	1
FR	2
GB	19
JP	185
KR	5
NO	3
SE	1
TW	6
US	437

E X H I B I T   4 . 3   **Priority Patent Countries**

for illustration, if you investigate the point below on the Samurai Sword and Japan, you will find it has truth.

Japan, which likewise has advanced transportation sciences to include aeronautical research, also has a history and tradition of precision metal refinement. (In fact, this tradition could be said to date back hundreds of years to the precision crafted Samurai Sword.)

This is not the only example of distant history having some bearing on present markets. Consider the entire German and Swiss chemical and pharmaceutical industry. It traces back to the English chivalry in the Middle Ages wanting brighter-colored textiles that local English textile makers proved unwilling to develop.

Patent citations analysis below, in almost all instances, confirms what you should already know. This statement does not apply to literature citations, which tell considerably more than patent citations (see Exhibit 4.4).

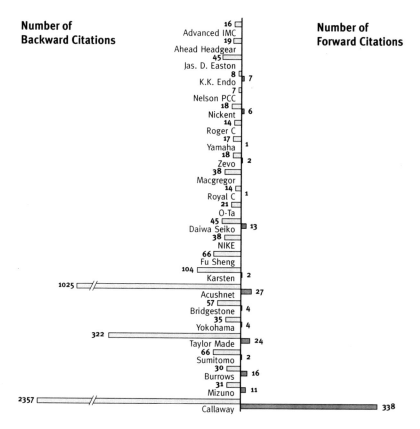

Number of Backward Citations

Number of Forward Citations

E X H I B I T   4 . 4   **Patent Profile**

Patent Citations

The patent citation profile in Exhibit 4.4 is consistent with the profile of a contested field in which most inventions are incremental improvements over previous inventions . . .

Companies provide the resource pool for inventors to work and the means to have their expertise reach a market. A patent analysis often profiles inventions in context with the owning organization.

Profile of Top Three Patenting Companies

Callaway Golf Company is the world's largest manufacturer of golf clubs. Its intention from its published corporate goals is to provide golf club heads capable of allowing even beginners to play golf with ease. It gained prominence in the market with its oversized Big Bertha clubs that Callaway's use of titanium made possible. The company's patent profile comprises documents that describe:

- Golf club sets with a large tolerance for error on the part of the user.
- Methods to afford favorable weight characteristics . . .
  - Prominent patent documents: US6475102B2, US6244976B1, US6238302B1
  - Most recent patent documents: US6932716B2, US6893358B2, WO2005023374A2

People create inventions. Unless it is not requested, any patent analysis that does not include information on key inventors, even if just to identify who they are, is incomplete. Tell users of the report something about the inventors behind key inventions.

Top Inventor Teams

Callaway Golf Company:

- Evans, Clayton
- Jacobson, Daniel R.
- Cackett, Matthew T.
- Rollinson, Augustin W.
- Reyes, Herbert

- Murphy, James M.
- Helmstetter, Richard C.
- Galloway, Andrew
- Hockneil, Alan

Taylor Made Golf Company, Inc.:

- Wahl, Bret
- Anderson, David
- Vincent, Benoit . . .

You may wish to add information that describes the nature of a research team's efforts.

Profile of Inventor Teams

Evans, Jacobson, Cackett, Rollinson, Reyes, Murphy, Helmstetter, Galloway, and Hockneil at Callaway Golf have worked on golf club heads made with titanium or steel faces of varying thickness with metal or composite aft materials. Additional innovations include a metal strip in the ribbon section of the club to provide favorable weight characteristics without affecting the structural durability and balance of the golf club head . . .

Conclusion

Tell the reader what you just told them. Then add a little more. Include at least one paragraph that addresses the search recipient's objective directly. Based on your business or technical analysis, should your customer pursue or not pursue a certain of action, and why?

The primary objective of golf club head research is to enhance the performance and experience of golf players. Golf club head designers walk a fine line between providing every possible advantage to players yet keeping golf club heads within PGA standards designed to keep play reasonably fair. Inventions revolve around making a golf ball consistently travel true and farther for both novices and experienced players. Upon investigating golf club patents, inventions to do the following proved the most common . . .

The final report should include a dataset so that recipients can, at a minimum, find patent references cited in the text or illustrated elsewhere in the report. An example appears in Exhibit 4.5.

US6354962 B1

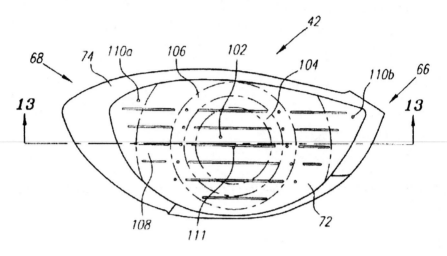

E X H I B I T   4 . 5   Patent #us6354962 B1

Patent Abstracts Associated with the Study

US6354962 B1
Golf club head with a face composed of a forged material
Callaway Golf Company

ABSTRACT

A golf club having a club head with a striking plate having a thickness in the range of 0.010 to 0.250 inches is disclosed herein. The club head may be composed of three pieces: a face, a sole, and a crown. Each of the pieces may be composed of a titanium material. The striking plate of the club head may have an aspect ratio less than 1.7. The striking plate may also have concentric regions of thickness with the thickness portion in the center. The club head may be composed of a titanium material, have a volume in the range of 175 to 400 cubic centimeters, a weight in the range of 165 to 300 grams, and a string plate surface area in the range of 4.00 to 7.50 square inches. The golf club head may also have a coefficient of restitution greater than 0.8 under test conditions such as the United States Golf Association (USGA) test conditions specified pursuant to Rule 4-1e, Appendix II, of the Rules of Golf for 1998–1999.

Inventor(s)

- Galloway, J. Andrew
- Helmstetter, Richard C.
- Hocknell, Alan
- Boyce, Ronald C.
- Aguinaldo, Homer E.
- Woolley, Curtis S.

Application No. 09/431982, **Filed** 19991101, **Granted** 20020312
U.S. Class: 473342
473345 473349
Int'l Class: A63B05304
A63B05306 A63B05308

CHAPTER 5

Approaches to Reporting Search Results

This chapter discusses the importance of communicating search results in ways that are comprehensive and informative, but not detrimental to the legal standing of a case. More than any other concept, the approach taken to reporting should be customized according to the requirements of the search recipient. Nevertheless, this chapter presents well-received approaches to the reporting of results.

An important purpose of patent searching is to provide technical interpretations of the prior art necessary to create legal opinions about the search subject matter. After the searching is performed and the search result set is final, the searcher usually will need to communicate the results to someone with the appropriate legal expertise (unless you are that person). A clear and informative reporting style is vital to the quality of the search and to the ease with which the attorney can then interpret the legal aspects of the subject matter of the invention, patent, or product in question.

The first section of this chapter presents a range of options and tools for designing a search report with the legal audience in mind. Each search report should be customized for the reader based on the context of the search and the specific requirements of the user. Ultimately, you will decide what to report based on the objectives of the search recipient (the person who commissioned the search).

Purpose of the Search Report

The patent search report serves two primary purposes: to present and discuss the relevant results, and to record the complete and accurate history of the search. If you are conducting the search for another person, you should present the findings in a clear and accessible format.

We have found the following approach to be welcomed by many patent practitioners at both companies and law firms. Whether you follow it and in what order is your prerogative.

The first aim of presenting and discussing results is often addressed by summary and reference discussion sections in the report. These sections are commonly included at the beginning of the search report. Because of the need to communicate information in an easily comprehensible format, these sections must concisely present discussions and analysis of the prior art that will assist the formulating of a legal opinion. These sections serve as an at-a-glance impression of the relevant content of the prior art.

The second part of the search report, a complete search history, contains detailed methodology information. The search report must delineate the boundaries of the searched subject matter clearly, so that the reader can comprehend the scope of the search. The level of detail should be such that the user would be able to replicate the search exactly as it was performed the first time. Furthermore, the search history serves to show "due diligence" in locating prior art.

The results of a patent search will contribute to the drafting of a legal opinion. However, experienced patent counsel will consider many factors when drafting an opinion. These factors include the purpose of the opinion,[1] the attorney's audience, his or her interpretations of case law, review of the patent prosecution history, and, finally, the results of the prior art search itself. Consequently, the searcher should refrain from offering legal advice about the relevance of any reference unless he or she is a patent attorney charged with that task.

Searchers naturally rely on their own interpretation of the search subject features and reference content in order to determine whether uncovered references are relevant to the search. However, the discussion of these selected results should be limited to objective facts about reference content and supported by citations from the document. It is always up to the legal experts to judge the relevance based on the content of the document. The searcher should limit his or her reporting to drawing out similarities between the search subject matter and the reference, in light of his or her understanding of the technical field.

ANATOMY OF A SEARCH REPORT

How to report the results of a search is not governed by a strict set of rules. The discussions that follow are intended to provide a general template for report format and content and do not need to be limited by the details and specifics shown as examples in this chapter. For instance, the results discussed in the sections below are presented in a table format, and subject feature and claim mapping features appear in the right-hand column for easy reference. It would have been just as effective and functional to summarize references in paragraph format and to present these mapping features in its section, in a table, or even just to organize references by the subject features. The important idea is to keep the end user's needs and expectations in mind when designing and customizing reports.

Although format and presentation may vary, most search reports contain four fundamental elements critical to communicating the methodology and results of the search: (1) summary, (2) subject matter, (3) discussion of references, and (4) search history.

WRITING A SUMMARY

The summary usually states the intent of the search and highlights the major results. The purpose of the summary is to provide context for the reader in reviewing the search report; it is not to provide a detailed description of the search strategy. An effective summary will briefly communicate the fundamental facts of the search: the subject matter; the kinds of prior art collections searched; and, when applicable, the critical dates limiting the scope such as for validity searches. A second reason for restating search scope is that, although these issues may have been agreed upon with the recipient before or during the search, it is likely that the end user may not be the only person to review the results. By including these details, another person who reviews the summary months or years later will understand the objectives and boundaries of the search.

After stating the basics, the summary will include the discussion of the results of the search. It is helpful to indicate the pertinent references, explain what features the art communicates, and identify which search subject features are lacking. Additionally, it is often useful to make descriptive statements about the results of the search. For example, the searcher might state that "three references were found to disclose two of the subject matter features" and "one reference was found to disclose all three subject matter features." This high-level summary will be supported by the more detailed discussions of references and can give the reader insights into what the searcher observed and found during the search. Presenting the reader with the objective and pertinent information of the search will make the search results comprehensible at a glance. For example, the summary may include the following:

> The subject of the search was a titanium bicycle seat to be mounted over the rear wheel of a bicycle, supported by members connected to the rear wheel axle, thus allowing a second person to ride as a passenger. The search was conducted for U.S. patents and published applications in the USPTO EAST database, and EP, PCT, GB, and DE patents and published applications, and JP published applications, were searched using Micropatent PatentWeb. Nonpatent literature was also searched using the Internet, Dialog, and IP.com.
>
> In general, the analyst found a number of references that disclosed second seats for bicycles, however many of these disclosed either seats to be attached between the user and the handlebars, or seats to be attached to the handlebars themselves. WO 9799999 discloses a basket for carrying groceries or other items over the rear wheel, to be mounted by members extending from the rear wheel axle. U.S. 4,444,444 discloses a seat mounted behind the user, where second seat extends from the same mounting bar as the primary seat and is not supported by members attached to the rear axle.
>
> U.S. 4,333,444 was identified by the client as known art and was therefore omitted from the search results. However, forward and backward citations of the reference were investigated.

PRESENTING THE SUBJECT MATTER

The search report may contain a list of search subject features, or a similarly detailed description of the search topic. The distinction between a summary of the search focus and a precise statement of the search subject matter is critical to understanding of the scope of the search. Suppose the search subject matter was presented in the report in summary style:

This search was performed on underwater rooms made from two-foot thick Plexiglas®, reinforced by regularly spaced 4-foot thick Kevlar®-reinforced Plexiglas® pillars to ensure there is no weakness at the joints of the Plexiglas® panels. The rooms are to be used for the viewing of tropical fish, where the rooms are part of an amusement park design with an aboveground section consisting of tide pool sea life exhibits.

This may be a thorough disclosure, but it does not explain the parameters of the search. For example, were only "underwater rooms" part of the search, or did the search for "reinforced Plexiglas® panels" (acrylic glass) extend to "glass-bottom boats"? Did the search strategy actually include documents related to aquariums or amusement parks, or did it focus only on reinforced acrylic glass?

To resolve the subject ambiguity, it is practical to present the subject features in a format that minimizes the chances of misinterpretation. A precise presentation of the search subject matter criteria might look like this:

1. An enclosed underwater space made at least partially from translucent material;

2. An underwater viewing space where the space is an underwater room or rooms made at least partially from translucent material, where the rooms are accessible from the surface;

3. An underwater viewing space or window made at least partially from translucent material, where the material is acrylic glass (Plexiglas®);

4. An underwater viewing space which is part of an amusement park or is used for recreational viewing of marine life; and

5. Any enclosed space or window made from Plexiglas®, where the adjoining Plexiglas® panels are reinforced by vertical or horizontal pillars molded over the adjoining faces of the panels, where the pillars are made from any suitable polymer material.

These subject matter features as presented here make the scope of the search apparent. Whoever commissioned the search will likely appreciate that the searcher approached the search looking both for documents related to any pillar-reinforced Plexiglas® structure, regardless of use, and for documents disclosing underwater viewing spaces used in amusement parks. These subject features do not imply that every patent document fulfilling the broadest feature will be included in the report, but they do imply that the searcher used varied search criteria to select references of possible significance in broad and related technological areas, rather than confining the search results only to documents pertaining to aquatic amusement parks with Plexiglas® rooms.

Presenting subject matter features in numbered or lettered format carries one particular advantage: numbering these subject features individually allows for the creation of a "spot check" column or table, by which the reader can quickly identify which references display which subject matter features with a visual indicator such as a check mark, X mark, or caret. For example:

Document Data	Discussion	Subject Features
U.S. 7,036,449 B2	Entertainment complex with both above-ground and underwater areas. Underwater observation and habitat areas are made from "bulletproof glass."	1◄ 2◄ 3◄ 4◄ 5
Man-made island resort complex with surface and underwater entertainment, educational and lodging facilities	[References throughout document. See especially description of Fig. 10, and claim 7]	
Sutter, Kimberly Michelle		
Granted May 2, 2006		

As discussed in the next section, a good discussion must support that the reference does indeed contain the indicated subject features, point out where in the reference the features can be found, and show how broadly or narrowly the subject features were interpreted by the searcher.

DISCUSSING REFERENCES

In order to present the content of results effectively, you as the searcher should know how the results will be used. Therefore, a general understanding of the usage of the search results by the attorney will lead to effective reporting and searching. What does a lawyer do with references and analysis once he or she receives them? To organize information so that it may quickly lead to a well-thought-out opinion, patent counsel might construct a summary chart as follows:

Bibliographic Data	Evidence from Reference	Feature of Subject Matter	Argument
U.S. 5,555,555 Mousetrap Smith Aug. 8, 1993	Claim 1. A mousetrap wherein the trigger platform is adapted to hold an attractive item that lures mice to trigger the spring mechanism.	The proposed invention of my client features a mouse pheromone that specifically lures mice to the trap, preventing roaches or other bugs from triggering the trap.	The specific application of pheromones to the platform is not covered by the "attractive item" language in claim 15; the claim states that the platform must be adapted to hold the item, indicating that it is intended to be a macroscopic physical object and not a chemical coating.

To help construct the preceding chart, the searcher will often interpret the features of the inventions or products disclosed in the literature and show that these features are related to the search subject matter features. In this case, a searcher was asked to perform a hypothetical infringement search on the proposed invention of the mousetrap that uses chemicals to lure mice. His reference discussion follows:

Document Data	Discussion
U.S. 5,555,555 A Mousetrap Smith, Jane Published Aug. 8, 1993	Reference discloses a mousetrap with spring-activated trigger platform adapted to hold an "attractive item" (claim 1). The example items that are discussed are cheese and seeds. The reference does not discuss a chemical or pheromone applied to the mousetrap. Figure 3, Paragraphs 15-16, Claim 1

A fundamental feature of all mousetraps is that mousetraps must entice the mouse to approach the trap. Therefore, the searcher approaches the search from the angle of investigating mousetrap patents that may claim the use of mouse pheromones, but the searcher should understand that infringement concerns could arise from a patent claiming a method of luring a mouse that is broad enough to cover pheromone use. When the searcher reports the results, it should be clear that the reference was selected because it contained claim 1, which is broad enough to cover "attractive items" used to lure mice. The searcher should show that this language may be related to the subject feature, even though it does not explicitly disclose mouse pheromones as the attractive aspect.

In constructing a legal argument from prior art, the patent professional must prove how the features of the product or invention in question are related to those features embodied in the prior art. The role of the searcher is to perform technical analysis to uncover potentially relevant references in light of the search subject matter, while refraining from making a legal opinion. This goal is accomplished through objective and factual discussions and presentations of evidences in the search report.

WRITING DISCUSSIONS

The discussion of the references is an important part of the search, and should be carefully written in order to be used and understood with the maximum benefit to the reader. The best discussions of patent documents are those that are short, concise, objective, and point to the features the documents disclose. The discussions give evidence to the reader that the document does indeed show the search subject features, show the reader how broadly or narrowly the searcher interprets the features, and show the reader exactly where to go in the reference to see the feature in context. A searcher may rely on the following guidelines to report the essential information:

- *Be concise but complete.* Avoid lengthy quotations from the document unless absolutely necessary. Instead, use your own words (supported by citations) to point to the features of interest in plain language. Discussions should report only relevant information; they should also be explicit as to what features are *not* shown in the document.

- *Be objective.* Like the summary, discussion sections are free-writing sections. The discussion sections should be entirely objective in tone, and they should be written as one would report facts, without embellishment or legal opinion.

- *Relate features.* One of the main purposes of the discussion is to show how the features described in identified literature were construed to relate to the search subject features. For example, a reference may discuss a feature in different, but possibly equivalent terms to those used in the subject disclosure. By showing the language from the reference and comparing it to that of the subject matter in the discussion section, the searcher can show how broadly the subject features were applied in evaluating references.

- *Present evidence.* The reference discussions should include a complete list of relevant passages and figures from the document. Because the end user will want to cite this evidence for his or her own case, identifying and interpreting these passages is an essential service to the client.

Example: Hamster Health Spa

Subject Features:

1. An exercise wheel for a small animal with a revolution counter to electronically record distance traveled.

2. An exercise wheel as in (1) where the revolutions are counted using a system involving laser beams.

3. An exercise wheel as in (1) where the laser beam is disrupted by a projection on the wheel and does not reach a sensor mounted opposite the cage, thus counting a revolution.

4. An exercise wheel as in (1) where insufficient revolutions during a set period of time triggers a motor to increase rotation speed for hamster training purposes.

5. An exercise wheel as in (1) where revolutions along with daily food and water consumption are recorded in a database and may be displayed graphically.

Document Data	Discussion	Subject Features
U.S. 0,000,000 A Revolution indicator for hamster exercise wheel J. P. Morgan Granted Nov, 2, 1999	Reference discloses a revolution counter for an exercise wheel suitable for a hamster. A detector records wheel revolution by using a laser detection system; a mirror is mounted on the wheel rim which reflects the laser beam into an optical sensor mounted on the cage. The revolutions do not trigger any motorized turning of the wheel to promote speed or endurance training for the hamster. See abstract, Figures 3, 5, and 6, columns 3–4, and claims 1–10.	1◄ 2◄ 3 4 5

The discussion describes the uncovered reference in terms of the search subject features by listing those that are found and that are not found. It concisely describes the key technical feature of the hamster wheel that differs from the one in the disclosure. It presents multiple citations as evidence for its assertion and for speedy reference, and it summarizes the present subject features in a spot-check column to the right. All these factors are designed to make it easy for the search recipient to quickly analyze the possible implications of the reference and to separate the results based on the useful subject features.

INDICATING CLAIMS

The way evidence is presented in the search report should differ based on the search type. Because claimed material takes on a special significance when performing infringement or validity searches, discussions for these searches should include claims information.

Clearance/Infringement/Right to Practice/Freedom to Operate: When discussing the search results for these types of searches, you should identify references containing material in the claims related to any of the subject features. The claims in a patent document provide the boundary of legal protection of the invention. Therefore, when reporting the results of a clearance- or infringement-type search, careful consideration should be taken to list the relevant claims for each central reference.

Document Data	Discussion	Subject Features	Related Claim(s)
U.S. 0,000,000	Example	1 ◄	5, 17, 24
Method of writing patent search reports	See col. 3, paragraph 15; claims 5, 17, 24, and 32.	2 3 ◄	32
Mary Smith		4	
May 5, 2003			

Validity: In a validity search, the related claims of the subject patent should be highlighted in the reference discussions. In many cases, the subject patent claims are listed as subject features. When the claims are extensive and the features of the claims are redundant, a consolidated set of appropriate subject features are used; in these cases, the discussion should specifically state all of the subject patent claims that may be related to the reference. In this case, the column used to display claims at a glance may be converted into a "Related to Subject Claims" column.

Document Data	Discussion	Subject Features	Related to Subject Claim(s)
U.S. 0,000,000 Method of writing patent search reports Mary Smith Filed Jan. 1, 2000 Issued May 5, 2003	Reference discloses a method of writing a search report beginning with a summary and ending with a complete search history. The disclosed search report will include all relevant information about identified references and contain concise analysis of each reference. See abstract, Figure 3, cols. 4–6.	1 ◄ 2 3 4 ◄	1–10, 12 15 (the claims in the patent under scrutiny for possible invalidity)

In addition, when reporting search results in validity studies, you should note that priority dates are very important. Presumably, before getting to the reporting stage, the search has been limited by a "cutoff date" agreed upon by the searcher and search recipient, often the earliest priority date of a patent application. A common request is for the search to include any U.S. patent filed before the critical date, and any foreign patent documents or nonpatent literature (NPL) published before the critical date. Therefore, when reporting search results, you should include both the filing and issue dates of the patent documents and applications.

PRIORITIZING REFERENCES

Format the report so that it provides the most relevant information. This is a logical extension of evaluating the references during the search itself. In Chapter 3, a method of evaluation was presented that placed highest priority on those references that disclosed multiple discrete subject features deemed central to the search focus; the method of prioritizing references presented here is based on the number and significance of the subject features that each reference discloses.

CENTRAL REFERENCES

The central references of the search results are usually those that most closely resemble the material of interest. Generally, any references that disclose the entire search subject features will be listed first, and the rest will be listed in descending order from the most to the least subject features disclosed. However, the order in which the references are displayed may be greatly changed depending on what type of search is being performed on the search subject matter.

Applying a different legal purpose to the same set of search results can significantly change the order of importance of the results. For example, consider a search on a topic with subject features A, B, and C. During a patentability (novelty) search, the analyst would be looking to provide the search recipient with either: (1) a reference that discloses a device with features A, B, and C; or (2) individual references disclosing A, B, and C separately, or in some combination. The logic behind this strategy is to provide the end user with material to anticipate (1) a novelty rejection or (2) a nonobviousness rejection of the proposed invention, respectively. A reference disclosing any invention with subject feature A, while useful, would not by itself complete these objectives, and so this reference would take a lower priority than one disclosing A, B, and C in combination. However, consider a clearance search performed on a proposed product with subject features A, B and C: a reference claiming a device with features A, B, D, E, and F, to be used in setting G, would take a lower priority in this report than a reference broadly claiming any device with subject feature A alone. If there were an existing in-force granted document that claimed the broad category of subject feature A as someone's intellectual property, that technology would surely need to be licensed from the owner before the product goes to market (or in some cases the inventor may choose to go back and design around the patented featured). So, as is seen from these examples, the difference between the concepts of patentability and product clearance (or infringement) causes a difference in the kind of result that is the most powerful when applied to the legal situation involved. This distinction is important to the search strategy and the reporting. These considerations should be remembered when identifying the subject features for the search; a well-defined search strategy further enables clear reporting.

PERIPHERAL REFERENCES

By following the evaluation method of Chapter 3, it may be that you have retrieved a number of references that can be said to disclose one or more search subject features, but also have run across a number of references that seem related to the search focus without actually disclosing any of the search subject features, or are too numerous to discuss in detail in the report. These references may be included in the search report as being peripherally related to the search. The reason behind this inclusion is to prevent accidental loss of relevant information: even if the recipient has approved the search strategy, you as the analyst may be interpreting the subject features in such a way that would exclude some references of peripheral interest; therefore, these references should also be noted for the report user's independent review and assessment.

The citing of peripheral art may also assist with the identification of additional embodiments. This broad approach to searching and reporting is especially useful given United States case law. Under current Federal Circuit case law, single embodiment disclosures in U.S. patents are often the cause of broad claims being either narrowly interpreted or held invalid for lack of written description support.

For example, in *Inpro II Licensing v. T-Mobile USA*, ___ F.3d ___, 2006 WL 1277815 (Fed. Cir. 2006), the term *host interface* in claims directed to a PDA (personal digital assistant) that interfaces with a host computer was construed to be limited to "a direct parallel bus interface," resulting in judgment of noninfringement by Blackberry PDAs that use serial bus interfaces. Why? Because, inter alia, "the only host interface described in the specification is a direct parallel bus interface."

In *LizardTech v. Earth Resource Mapping*, 424 F.3d 1336 (Fed. Cir. 2005), the court held that claims broadly reciting a method for seamlessly compressing, storing, and subsequently retrieving tiles of large digital images using DWT (discrete wavelet transform) technology, without reciting the specific step described in the specification for making the images seamless, were invalid for lack of § 112, ¶1 written description support. Why? Because, said the court, "the specification provides only a single way of creating a seamless DWT" (Id. at 1344).

While most patent professionals recognize the important roles that a good patent search serves in deciding whether to file a patent application and, if so, how to craft the claims and disclosure, another potential benefit of a broad search that seems to be overlooked is to search for prior art that provides ideas for alternative embodiments of inventions. It is often recommended to search not only the closest prior art, but also patents and publications that may be helpful in stimulating inventors to think of embodiments beyond that in the original invention disclosure.

CENTRAL AND PERIPHERAL REFERENCES

The division of results into sets of centrally and peripherally relevant references may occur naturally in the selection process. In many cases, this distinction will be easy to draw; most of the time, all references with at least one related subject feature would likely go in the central results, while all the patent documents that came close or were selected for other reasons would likely go in the peripheral results. However, there are occasions where very few references are found that disclose even one of the subject features, and situations in which there are pages and pages of references that disclose only one of the subject features of interest. When this occurs, you may wish to consult the person who commissioned the search in order to determine the best course of action.

Sometimes, the patent analyst will need to rely on his or her own discretion in deciding which references to highlight and which to deem peripheral. Some analysts, with a large number of references disclosing a particular subject feature, will consider these references as peripheral and place them in a separate section or table, and will note it in the report summary. This has the benefit of preventing the analyst from spending an inordinate amount of time discussing each reference or preventing the search recipient from receiving an overwhelming list of central references to consider.

There is one important rule when choosing which references will be highlighted and discussed in the report: you should consider the rarity of the subject features before assigning references to the peripheral table. For example, if the results for a search with four main subject features contain a dozen references each disclosing features 1, 2, and 3, and several dozen references only containing feature 1, but there are just two references containing subject feature 4 (alone), it may be appropriate to delegate the references containing feature 1 only into the peripheral results. Feature 1 is apparently so common that some of these references may even be excluded from the results set altogether. However, the two references containing subject feature 4, although they disclose only one subject feature, may be considered much more valuable to the search results. One of these two references may be a key missing piece that the search recipient can use to build a case.

Another situation that may arise, similar to the one previously discussed, is when many references are uncovered in a search for features A, B, and C, but all of the uncovered documents disclose only subject feature A. When most or all of the references have a seemingly similar relevance, it is helpful to choose a few and discuss them as exemplary references to give the reader the general idea of the best material found in the search. The complete search results may then be listed with bibliographic data only. Care may be taken to choose those references that disclose subject feature A for a particular use or in a particular setting that is similar to the intended one for the invention or product in question.

Search History

Finally, the last section of the report should contain a search history (the record of the approach taken to conducting the search). To ensure the usefulness of the search and its results, the search history must serve as a complete search record, so that the reader can be sure of exactly what material was searched for and where the analyst looked for it.

Some writers are tempted to include this in the first section of the report, as a justification for the results that follow; however, that kind of format hinders the readability of the report. Instead of asking the reader to immediately review a detailed search history, the more effective strategy is to present them with the significant findings of the search in a brief summary, lay out the subject matter of the search for context, and then to discuss the most important references. Once the reader understands what has been found, he can then refer to the search history at the end of the report (e.g., an appendix) to support and reinforce his confidence that the search was performed as completely as initially defined.

Because of its usefulness in re-creating the search at a later date, the search history should be a complete record of the searcher's methodology, from beginning to end. It should be detailed enough that a reader would be able to conduct the same search, in the same databases, with the same queries. A few elements are common to every complete search history.

CLASSIFICATION AREAS

As discussed in Chapter 3, classification searching is vital to the quality of a patent search. To give the reader assurance that you have searched in all relevant areas, search histories should contain a complete list of class and subclass definitions. The subclass definitions should also include the definitions of all the more major subclasses of which they are a part. For example, suppose the searcher performed a search in U.S. subclasses 316 and 318 in class 114:

Class 114	SHIPS
312	SUBMERSIBLE DEVICE
313	With disparate vehicle feature
314	Underwater habitat
315	Diver assistance device
316	With weapon or weapon system
317	Having ballast compensating means
318	Power assisted deployment
319	Pneumatic or hydraulic dispatch

Subclass 316 is listed under 312, "submersible devices," and subclass 318 is further listed under 316, "submersible devices with weapon or weapons system." For clarity and thorough reporting, the subclass definitions should include all of the applicable higher classifications:

Class	Subclass	Definition
114		SHIPS
	316	Submersible device; With a weapon or weapons system
	318	Submersible device; With a weapon or weapons system; Power assisted deployment

Databases Accessed

Each database contains unique collections, and the date coverage of these may vary (see Chapter 6). It may be that the subject matter topic is a very new concept, and that the search must include up-to-the-minute publications in order to represent the true state of the art. In this case, it is disadvantageous for a search to be conducted in a database known for lagging behind in current publications by weeks or even months.

However, the subject matter topic may be a simple mechanical concept. In this situation, it is likely that because the concept is simple, it is already represented back in the distant annals of patent art; it would therefore be appropriate to search in databases that contain the optical character recognition (OCR) text of U.S. patent publications before 1971. Because selection of the database to search impacts the coverage and quality of the search, this information must be disclosed in order for the search record to be complete.

For text searches and other limited searches, the search history should contain a record of the search strings used in the database, complete with other limiting parameters such as U.S. or international patent classification (IPC) subclass or date limitations. The records should also contain the number of hits and the individual collections within the database that were searched.

The searcher should copy search strings and paste them into the search report, so that the record of the search is as accurate as possible. If the reader, for instance, has a question about whether a synonym or an alternate spelling of a word was included in the search strategy, he or she will likely consult the search strings used.

Examiners Contacted

As discussed in Chapter 3, U.S. Patent and Trademark Office (USPTO) examiners may be contacted and will answer general questions about U.S. classification areas and in which subclasses to begin a search. It is useful for the reader to be aware of any guidance provided by an examiner.

Conclusion

The reporting formats and technique presented in this chapter are targeted to address the primary purposes of the search report: communicating important search results and recording a complete search history. The ideas presented here are tools and options designed to present relevant information in an easily accessible format, enabling the reader of the search report to efficiently investigate results based on a summary of the most important content. A well-written search report promotes confidence in the search and allows the search to be understood and reconstructed, if necessary. Whatever format is used, the writer should understand the needs and expectations of the reader.

Note

1. For example: validity, infringement, clearance, patentability, due diligence, or prelitigation.

CHAPTER 6

Search Tools

This chapter presents tips for comparing search engines and a discussion of data sources of both patents and nonpatent literature (NPL). It suggests criteria by which to select the most appropriate source for a particular search, and discusses several data sources at length. Fortunately, commercial data providers continually update their product offerings, so a comprehensive comparison of data coverage, prices, availability, and features is beyond the scope of this book. If it were to be included, the book would become outdated upon its date of publication.[1]

THE AVAILABILITY OF PATENT INFORMATION

Patent information is available from both free and fee-based sources. Most free sources are sponsored by government patent authorities, such as the U.S. Patent and Trademark Office (USPTO, www.uspto.gov) and the European Patent Office (EPO, www.espacenet.com). These sites allow users to search and retrieve patents for that authority and often, other countries. A search of a country's official Web site sometimes yields the most thorough results for that authority's pending and issued patents. Unfortunately, most government Web sites are not well suited for advanced searching and a fee-based service is essential for the professional searcher. The best sources are subscription based and provide extensive coverage of international patent documents. Although there are many patent databases, the more common ones include:

- IFI Patent Intelligence
- Jouve PatAnalyst
- Micropatent Patent Web
- Minesoft Pat Base
- Patent Café ICO Suite (Intellectual Capital Office)
- Questel-Orbit QPAT and QWEB
- Thomson Delphion
- Thomson Derwent World Patent Index (DWPI)
- Thomson Dialog
- Lexis Nexis
- Univentio

Stephen Adams has written a book that provides an overview of patent search engines and their capabilities, titled *Information Sources in Patents*, 2nd completely new edition (K.G. Saur, 2005) and is an excellent resource.

Juan Carlos Vergara, Allessandro Comai, and Joaquin Tena Millan have written a survey, titled *Software for Technological Intelligence*, (EMECOM, 2006) that evaluates various software systems and tools used to conduct in-depth patent analysis. It is a good resource for understanding some of the more sophisticated analytical tools used by the patent community.

CRITERIA FOR SELECTING SEARCH TOOLS

Before entering search terms into a query, there are a number of factors that must be addressed to ensure a suitable search. First, it is impossible to declare one engine superior to all others. Depending on your needs, a database that is useful for one type of search might be ill equipped to handle another.

When selecting the correct patent search tool, we recommend comparing the available data sources against your set of objectives. Your objectives will differ depending on your language, your technical specialty, your search skills, your budget, and your specific type of project (e.g., prior art search vs. patent landscape study). Nevertheless, we offer the following criteria to help you to compare the patent databases and search engines of competing providers. You will likely add criteria to suit your objectives.

Data Coverage

Data coverage is the number of patent documents (both patents and published patent applications) that are included in the database and are searchable. The vendor should be asked to list what patent authorities (countries) are covered in the database, the kinds of patents included (A1, B1, C, etc.), the exact dates of coverage, and any and all discrepancies in the data. This is an important task because all patent data providers will tell you what their product has, but few will tell you what their product does not have, unless asked. For example, a data provider may tell you that their system has Korean patents from "1988 to the present." Upon further questioning, you might find that the coverage begins on March 30, 1988, and ends on a date two months ago. It does not have patents for all of 1988 nor recently issued patents that have yet to be uploaded into their system. In addition, you might find upon questioning that the database is missing patents from September 1, 1989, through October 31, 1989. This would be a problem if an invalidating patent issued in late September 1989 and you did not search it.

For example, Micropatent PatentWeb is an exceptional product with many features. However, Micropatent currently has European granted patents back to 1980 and gaps in its European published applications. On its Web site, the company has stated that "approximately 13,300 European application records published from 1978 to 1988 are missing from the full text database."

Document Delivery

Document delivery is the method and format by which you may view, download, print, and save patent documents (both images and text). Most data providers permit you to retrieve documents in a common file format (e.g., Adobe PDF). When working with large data sets, you will want the ability to download more than one patent document at a time. Therefore, the vendor should permit batch downloads of documents easily and quickly and, if possible, at no additional expense. This is often accomplished with a zip function that compresses the patent documents for fast transmission over the Internet.

Import and Export Functions

Several data providers permit you to view and export the text of patents in a datasheet for use in another software program. A datasheet is a spreadsheet or database of patent documents. This is a good feature to have when you are analyzing large data sets, when exporting them to a visualization tool (e.g., Vantage Point), or for creating a database of relevant patents for a specific project.

The ability to *export* patent data is an important feature when selecting a patent database provider. You should insist that the system you select has the capability to export patent data into a commonly used format (e.g., .xls, .csv, .mdb). The ability to *import* data is essential to a data visualization tool, such as Derwent Analytics, Micropatent's Aureka, or Vantage Point. The reason is that most patent analysts are already aware of at least some patents that interest them prior to conducting an in-depth analysis or competitive intelligence. They may have a database or a spreadsheet of their own company's patents and do not need to use a search system to locate them. They may have even retrieved the dataset from a patent search system that was built by a company other than the provider of the visualization software. Therefore, all quality patent visualization tools will allow you to import a dataset, and, if not, the vendor should be pressed to provide this capability.

Finally, most patent visualization tools accept imports of patent data from the search system provided by that same developer. This approach is fine if you intend to purchase access to that company's patent search system and patent database. However, that provider must also permit imports from other sources or their system will be inadequate for your needs and, in fact, will force you to use a patent search engine that you may not want to use.

Pricing

Patent data providers have adjusted their prices in recent years primarily by not charging additional for patent copies and by offering less expensive site licenses for large customers. When negotiating price, there are a few guidelines to remember.

You should question the data provider on the costs to permit multiple user access to their system. You should also question what the charges would be to renew your license at the end of its term, annually or otherwise. This is critical because some vendors will show a low price up front and not discuss the cost of renewing your license, obtaining discounts for additional users, or obtaining a site license. The better data providers will include training and some customer service support for no additional charge for at least some time period.

Competition has increased among patent data providers, so it is possible to lower your access costs through negotiation. In order to succeed, however, you will need to know who the primary patent database competitors are and the capabilities of their respective systems.

Usability

Usability is an assessment of how easy it is to learn and use the system. With few exceptions, search systems that are easy to use will improve your efficiency. Data providers affect the usability of their systems by the placement of menu items, icons, and buttons; by the number of steps required to execute a command; by which portions of a patent may be displayed or displayed simultaneously (e.g., ability to view the abstract, main drawing figure, and the independent claims all at once); the ability of the user to control which parts of a patent may be displayed at any time; the option for more experienced searchers to bypass menu items and search by command line; ability to store and modify queries, alerts, and monitors in a search session or indefinitely; ability to e-mail or share search results; and others. In our view, the data providers that truly address usability beyond "bells and whistles" will best position themselves for success as the increasingly competitive patent search system market becomes commoditized. In any event, you should demand easy-to-use and easy-to-learn systems, as your time is valuable.

Company Strength

You should consider the management and market strength of the provider prior to purchasing access to their patent or nonpatent literature search system. This criterion does not mean that you need to conduct a business or financial analysis of the company in question. It does mean that you should read the company's Web site, locate discussion groups, solicit feedback on the data provider from objective parties, determine the level of customer support provided by the provider, and research how long that data source has been publicly available without interruption. This criterion is best illustrated with an example. Recently, we compared the patent search systems of four companies at a conference in Europe. The most impressive system was offered by a small firm that had the backing of a large, established public company. Shortly before we were about to sign the agreement to license the system for use, we discovered that the company had no support staff in the United States (our home), erratic business hours, and no timetable for product improvements. We also determined that the system was a collaboration of three companies with no company that seemed fully responsible for its current or future development. The system's technical features were impressive; everything else was not.

WHEN TO SELECT A SEARCH TOOL

The patent searcher should understand when a particular search tool should be used. For example, it is more productive to search patent information before technical publications in more established, slower-evolving technologies such as the mechanical arts. This is because "older" technologies have years of patent activity that can be searched and usually fewer unpublished patent applications than very active fields, such as biotechnology. It is more productive to begin a mechanical search in a patent database prior to searching nonpatent literature (NPL).

By contrast, biotechnology is a highly innovative field. Patent applications are filed frequently and the industry often publishes its research findings in trade journals. Many of the journal articles are printed and available to the public prior to the publishing of the corresponding patent application. Therefore, the biotechnology patent searcher should consult NPL as often as patents.

Patent search tools vary in data coverage, price, and purpose. Some systems have graphical user interfaces (GUIs) while some use command-line prompt systems. Most rank and prioritize the user's inputs and output the resulting "hits" or applicable patent or nonpatent literature to the user.

The core purpose of an engine is to systematically parse the volumes of literature—through a user's calculated entry of search terms. A search engine must therefore provide an all-encompassing breadth and depth of a desired subject matter. Included in this coverage is a need for a large range of dates, geographic variety, and ways of using these characteristics to quickly find pertinent references.

Breadth and Depth of Data Coverage

Two important features of a patent search engine are (1) its breadth of data coverage and (2) the ability for a user to display only those references that meet well defined search criteria. The breadth of data coverage is important because missing one critical patent reference from a search could be legally and financially disastrous for the search recipient. The ability to display references based on refined search criteria is important because patent searchers are not always given the time to read and analyze thousands of patent references for every search.

There are several ways to limit the scope of a search. A patent analyst may limit the scope with date delimiters, the exclusion of certain patent authorities, inventorship, a search of only portions of the patent document, and others. Following is an example of how a search might be limited in scope depending on the nature and exhaustiveness of the request. It is presented for illustrative purposes only:

Sample parameters	Example
Patent filing dates	1999 to 2001
Patent authorities	U.S., EPO, JP
Proximity of search terms	"Digital" within three words of "print*"
Inventor	Jones not Harold

In addition to having many ways of parsing documents, it is important that a search tool be inclusive of divergent subject matters. For example, the parameters used in a mechanical patentability search on "clothespins" would not translate well to another application in, for example, a biotechnology search on "nanotubes." Regardless of the search, the tool should accommodate the breadth of the particular subject matter being searched, because a search is not coextensive across art lines.

DATA SOURCES FOR CHEMICAL SEARCHES

The currency of the scientific community is literary publication in scientific journals. Therefore, a comprehensive chemical search will include a review of both patent and nonpatent literature. In fact, it is not uncommon for the most relevant art to be located among the technical publications shortly after a scientist has filed for patent protection.

STN is a conduit for many specialty databases including Biosis, CAPlus, and Medline. STN provides access to volumes of nonpatent publications through these and other databases.

Biosis contains abstracts and indexed information from reportedly 5,500 global sources on topics that range from botany to genetic engineering. CAPlus, produced by Chemical Abstracts Service (CAS), reportedly contains 24 million patent and journal article references in subjects ranging from organic chemistry to biochemistry. Medline, produced by the U.S. National Library of Medicine, reportedly contains 12 million citations from 4,600 biomedical journals published in the United States and other countries.

STN is a good resource for conducting chemical structure, nucleic acid, and protein sequence searches. Specifically, the STN Registry file displays all substance records that contain a unique CAS Registry Number®. Substance records may have CA index names, synonyms, molecular formulas, alloy composition tables, classes for polymers, protein and nucleic acid sequences, ring analysis data, and structure diagrams—all of which may be searched and displayed.[2] A user can enter the structure, nucleic acid sequence, or protein sequence and search the registry file for all known records that contain the queried substance. The resulting "hits" may be "crossed into" CAPlus to retrieve related journal articles.

Professional patent searchers often use CAPlus to search chemical structures but consult other resources when searching nucleotide sequences and amino acid sequences.

The National Center for Biotechnology Information (NCBI) is a sufficient resource for a cursory search of sequences. Established in 1988 as a resource for molecular biology information, NCBI creates public databases, conducts research in computational biology, develops software tools for analyzing genome data, and disseminates biomedical information.[3] The Web site's "BLAST" tool permits a search of nucleic acid and amino acid sequences, but omits many records due to a lack of international content and the inability to construct advanced searching algorithms when using its search engine. Nevertheless, the resource is free and can provide adequate coverage of the NPL depending on your needs.

A more powerful tool, used by USPTO examiners, is the Automated Biotechnology Sequence Search (ABSS) System. ABSS provides coverage of commercially available databases such as Genbank/EMBL, Geneseq, PIR, and UniProt. This resource permits routine and specialized sequence searching, including alignments, length-limited, oligomer, and score/length.[4]

Biocceleration Inc. (www.biocceleration.com) provides this resource to commercial entities, and the software requires subscriptions to Geneseq (DWPI's sequence repository with sequence flat files). The GCG format of all publicly available sequence data is required prior to using the ABSS system. The power of ABSS is enormous compared to BLAST. Apart from the greater sensitivity of the Smith-Waterman sequence alignment algorithm it uses, BLAST is extremely limited as to supported parameter sets. For example, if you attempt to adjust its parameters in order to perform a fragment search known as an "oligo" search, the NCBI program will not accept the changes and displays a message saying that those parameters are not supported.

In addition to ABSS, a less expensive alternative, although not providing international coverage, is a new file formed through a partnership of SequenceBase Corporation and FIZ Karlsruhe offers STN file "USGENE." The file covers all peptide and nucleic acid sequences from the published applications and issued patents of the USPTO from 1982 to date. This product was unavailable to test prior to this printing; however, the company's press accounts tout many valuable features:

> USGENE is the new unparalleled resource for freedom-to-operate, prior art, validity and infringement patent sequence searches; Competitive analysis of organizations with biosequence patents; Current awareness alerts (SDIs) from the very latest USPTO sequence data.[5] The USGENE file includes three advanced sequence searching methods; NCBI BLAST®, the FastA-based GETSIM, and GETSEQ for fragment sequences or motif sequence queries. The database also provides fully searchable organism name, sequence length, publication sequence identity number (SEQ ID NO) and feature tables for modifications and other features. USGENE database includes extensive bibliographic and text search options, including publication title, abstract, full patent claims, patent assignees at issue, full inventor names, plus the complete set of publication, application and parent case WIPO/PCT numbers and dates. Single-click full-text links from USGENE sequence records to USPTO original documents on the web are available to all searchers using STN Express® with Discover! and STN on the Web.

There are a many other data providers and publisher-affiliated search engines available to the professional searcher, whose selection will depend on the user's budget and needs.

Advanced Chemical Development Labs (ACD/Labs) (www.acdlabs .com) provides ChemSketch, which is a program that allows you to draw a structure and view it in 3D. This program can also provide names for these structures in cases where you have the picture of the structure but not the name. This can give you a quick and easy way of acquiring information. ChemSketch is free to use, but not all of the features are available in the free version. Still, the free version is a powerful tool for biochemical and pharmaceutical researches alike.

Data Sources for Mechanical Searches

In contrast to the chemical search that potentially spans both patent and nonpatent literature databases, a good mechanical search can depend more heavily on the body of patent literature. Unlike newer technologies, the mechanical arts were practiced in 1790 at the inception of the U.S. Patent Office. Therefore, useful mechanical search tools will include older patent documents.

The length of coverage depends on the search tool. Micropatent Patent-Web, a fee-based service, displays full text information from 1836; the date the first numerically cataloged U.S. patent was issued.[6] Delphion offers the full text and images of all patents issued by the USPTO since 1974, and bibliographic text and some images since 1971. Delphion's granted U.S. patent collection includes images for backfile patents dated 1790–1971.[7]

If you are located in the Washington, D.C., metropolitan area, you may access the USPTO's EAST search system, which is located in the Madison Building in Alexandria, Virginia. This patent search system is also available under the name WEST at three of the agency's patent depository libraries in Sunnyvale, California; College Station, Texas; and Detroit, Michigan. Alternatively, you may conduct a search at the PTO's Web site at www.uspto.gov. All of the USPTO approaches are free and permit you to view U.S. patent documents back to 1790. There are missing patents from the collection due in part to a fire that ravaged the office in 1836.[8] However, full-text documents that are missing from the collection may be found at www.uspto.gov/patft/help/contents.htm.

The USPTO Web site allows word searching of various parts of the patent and provides guidance to the patent searcher on how to search effectively. The full text of patent documents may be searched from 1976 to the present. The full texts of pre-1976 patents are not available, and so the original scans must be searched by patent number, issue date, or current U.S. classification number. In order to view patent images on the USPTO Web site, tagged image file formats (TIFFs) must be enabled or added to the Internet browser. The software driver can be found at www.alternatiff .com.

The USPTO Web site displays only U.S. patents and published applications; however, the on-site system, EAST, allows you to search the patent documents of the EPO, the Japanese Patent Office (JPO), and Derwent records.

Another critical requirement for the mechanical search is the availability of figures in a patent database. Using a tool like EAST, a mechanical searcher can scan through a list of patents in an image browser that displays only the figures of each published application or patent. Thus, the need to laboriously read through the specifications and claims is eliminated. While the claims define the invention, the figures will often convey the inventive concept and can be easily compared to other figures to more efficiently determine novelty.

There are several approaches to searching nonpatent literature in the mechanical arts. The fee-based service Compendex reportedly has a catalog of "5,000 scholarly journals, trade magazines and conference proceedings, containing over eight million records." Compendex is updated weekly and reports that 500,000 records are added annually.[9] The database covers the general, civil, chemical, mechanical, electrical, civil engineering, materials science, and energy fields.

The National Technical Information Service (NTIS) database is a well-known source for accessing unclassified reports from influential U.S. and international government agencies. Reportedly, two million critical report citations may be viewed from U.S. government departments and include the National Aeronautics and Space Administration (NASA), the United States Department of Energy (DoE), the German Federal Ministry of Research and Technology, the U.S. Department of Defense (DoD), and the Japan Ministry of International Trade and Industry (MITI).[10]

It is critical than any system used for mechanical searches display early-issued patents and contain both full-text data and images. Mechanical searches, more than any other type of technical field, require analysis of any part of a patent.

DATA SOURCES FOR
ELECTRICAL/COMPUTER SEARCHES

Patent Data Sources for Electrical and Computer Searches

The difference between a mechanical and an electrical search is not clear to the uninitiated. Harnessing radio waves and computational machines was formerly considered electrically based subject matter. These concepts are now considered mechanical inventions, as are light bulbs, phonographs, and older types of telephones. In fact, the rapid pace of advancements in electronics and electrical engineering (EE) require the professional searcher to be ever aware of changes in technologies and how to search them.

With the rise of Asian economies, the professional searcher will often need to search the text of Japanese, Korean, and Taiwanese patent documents. This is essential for electronics, EE, and computer hardware searches.

A free resource is the JPO Web site (www.jpo.go.jp). The JPO site is unique in that it allows the user to execute a machine translation of Japanese full-text patent documents. In fact, many English speaking electrical searchers use this site as an inexpensive translator of full-text JP patent data. Alternatively, Japanese and English language versions of the Japanese-based fee-based search system, Patolis (www.patolis.co.jp), are superb.

A European product, PatAnalyst (www.patanalyst.com), has a large collection of patent abstracts of Asian countries. For bibliographic data and abstracts, PatAnalyst reportedly has Japanese documents from 1928, Korean documents from 1978, Taiwanese documents from 1983, and Chinese documents from 1985. PatAnalyst also reportedly provides the full text of U.S. patents from 1836. PatAnalyst will yield many JP documents, but provides the searcher with only translated abstracts. By contrast, the JPO Web site provides a *full-text* machine translation.

NPL Sources for Electrical Searches

As with biotechnology, the fast-paced evolution of electronics and EE creates the need to search NPL. Fee-based databases, such as Compendex and NTIS, are useful search tools. Inspec, a service of the British Institution of Engineering and Technology (IET)[11] is a valuable resource for EE content. According to the provider, "Inspec is the world's leading bibliographic database providing comprehensive global coverage of scientific and technical literature in the fields of physics, electrical engineering, electronics and computer science."[12] In addition, the IEEE/IET Electronic Library (IEL), produced by the Institute of Electrical and Electronics Engineers (IEEE) and the Institution of Engineering and Technology (IET), reportedly "provides access to almost a third of the world's current electrical engineering and computer science literature."[13]

DATA SOURCES FOR BUSINESS METHODS SEARCHES

In July 1998, a federal court upheld a patent for a method of calculating the net asset value of mutual funds.[14] After this date, an increasing number of U.S. patents have been issued to companies that have devised novel ways of doing business. These patents, which usually combine software with business methodology, are commonly referred to as *business method patents.*

These patents serve a particular niche in the society and an increasingly important one. They are important because they protect any business method a company patents from use by another company for 20 years, thereby allowing the company that possesses the patent to market the technology to other companies for a fee.

One overused example of a business method patent is the "one-click" ordering process owned by Amazon.com. Amazon developed the one-click system, which allows the consumer to bypass the arduous task of filling in customer information once established in the customer database. Amazon was granted the patent on this business method in September 1999 (U.S. 5,960,411).

The search of business methods can be difficult due to the fact that much of the technology is new and not already patented. A good tool for conducting a business methods search is a meta-search engine because of its access to many databases.

Often, cutting-edge research is conveyed through NPL. Patents can take months to years to be made available to the public, while many new software, Internet, and business tools and processes are disclosed daily in newspapers, journals, and on the Web. These are the best sources for locating prior art in the rapidly developing areas of business methods.

Many patented business methods relate to financial and business data processing. They are often illustrated as images of figures or flowcharts in the patent search engines. No business method search is thorough without a search of NPL and information located on the Internet. This is because a specific business method can have applicability across many business applications that are not easily classified.

The USPTO has acknowledged the difficulty of effectively covering the body of publicly available NPL when conducting a search. In 2000, the PTO issued an action plan to help examiners and the public improve the quality of their business methods searches. PTO guidelines enumerated mandatory searching policies for examiners. These require subclass and key word searches and a search of NPL. The search of technical literature (all nonpatent sources) should be related to US Class 705. The NPL search should also include "all appropriate databases from among nine hundred (900) databases specifically listed (e.g., Software Patent Institute [SPI], IEEE/IEE Electronic Library [IEL Online], etc.)."[15]

Publicly available submissions to other government agencies can also be used as prior art, and one such repository of these submissions relevant to business methods can be found in the U.S. Securities and Exchange Commission's Electronic Data Gathering Analysis & Retrieval (EDGAR) database.[16] Therefore, EDGAR is a good resource for conducting business methods searches and is available for free (www.sec.gov/edgar) from the U.S. government and for a fee from commercial data providers. A good fee-based service is Global Securities Information's LivEdgar (www.livedgar.com), which is available to occasional users for a few thousand U.S. dollars per year.

In addition, Web sites and software products can be used as prior art, provided that they were "first installed" or "released" and publicly available more than one year prior to applicant's filing date. An inherent difficulty of using Web sites as references and their normally "up-to-date" nature is the ability to find an "old" Web site or a record of when a subject matter was first posted on a particular site.

In order to establish early Web site dates, a searcher can use commercial databases or a resource known as the "Wayback machine." A commercial database can be used in the sense that a periodical citing a Web site can reveal the age of the site or, worst-case scenario, the publication date of the article can be used. However, only the content relied upon in the article from the site can receive the benefit of the publication's information or date.

Another method of finding the earliest versions of Web sites (back to 1996) is to use the site www.archive.org/. This Internet archive maintains previously posted versions of the pages from the World Wide Web This site is available to the public for free. While the pages accessed may be archived, links on the archived page probably are further linked to current information. As a result, you should use caution when attempting to find the earliest date of public availability for a particular Web site.

METHODS OF ACCESS

Typically, the free Web sites that are available for searching are suffixed by ".org" or ".gov." A tool that is an example of such a free ".org" Web site having coverage from the first U.S. patent in 1836 to the present is www .pat2pdf.org. Though this Web site does not allow for any type of searching within the information of the patent, it is a helpful tool for obtaining a free copy of the patent.

TEXT SEARCH SYNTAX

Regardless of the engine used, a search is only as good as the parameters entered by the operator. The most comprehensive database will yield poor results if the searcher does not input the proper terms; in contrast, a minimally equipped engine in the hands of skilled searcher can find relevant art. While narrowing a broad subject matter with fields such as issue date, inventor, assignee, class/subclass, and so on helps to target applicable references, strategically placing search terms next to one another also proves useful. Patent and nonpatent literature resources allow the searcher to require for example that two words be a certain distance apart or in the same paragraph. For example, using EAST, the command "microfluidic same nucleic" requires that a result must have these two terms in the same paragraph within its text. Likewise, in STN, "microfluidic (5a) immobilize" requires that the two terms be five words adjacent to one another. It is important for a search tool to provide a searcher many ways of creating a context within which their terms are likely to appear.

Boolean commands, truncation, and proximity operators are implemented differently in the various search engines. Some engines presume, unless otherwise instructed, that a certain Boolean is placed between key-words, which is similar to a Google search. The PTO EAST system, for example, automatically has the operator "OR" placed between keywords. The query "elliptical circular uniform oblong" would be interpreted as "el-liptical OR circular OR uniform OR oblong." EAST is also capable of switching the automatic Boolean "or" for "and," "near," "andnot." "with" and "adj." By contrast, less sophisticated search engines allow only the general "and," "andnot," and "or" Booleans, such as the USPTO Web site and a less robust version of Dialog, sold as DialogPro.

The ability to end truncate a word is an essential. Using the last example, "microfluidic (5a) immobili?" requires that the two terms not only be five words adjacent to one another but also any variation of ending to the root "immobili" will be searched, that is, immobilization, immobilize, immo-bilised (British spelling), and so on. Also, beginning truncation allows for multiple permutations of a word. For example, using STN, the keyword "?array" will yield hits with "microarray," "DNA-array," and "gene-array."

Each search engine has a unique style and nomenclature when process-ing text search strings, but all are relatively easy to learn. The wildcard truncation symbol "★" (used with PatentWeb), "$" (used with EAST) and "?" (used with STN) are used to locate a variety of spellings of a word. A search engine that has the necessary and sufficient syntax abilities is one that combines many Boolean operators with selectable fields (date, author, claims), truncations, and proximity operators. Principally, each search en-gine is attempting to mimic the comparative processes that occur within a discerning human mind. These systems cannot understand the significance of the patents and nonpatents its finds, but the best tools expedite the iden-tification of relevant art.

DISCUSSION OF SPECIFIC SEARCH TOOLS

USPTO Search Room

The search facility at the USPTO provides public access to patent copies. The patents are organized by U.S. classification codes, which may be found online at www.uspto.gov or in hard copy in the reference room. The few keystrokes involved in typing ".ccls." in EAST and narrowing a search by classification is much simpler than physically leafing through the paper copies found in the USPTO library.

U.S. Patent and Trademark Depository Libraries (PTDL)

Though inadequate for the professional patent searcher, the United States has eighty PTDLs that house patent information. A PTDL is a physical library commissioned by the USPTO to house paper copies of U.S. patents, U.S. trademarks, and related materials, which are freely available to the public.

Every U.S. state except Arizona, Connecticut, and New Hampshire has at least one PTDL. In order to find one, visit the USPTO's Web site at www.uspto.gov/go/ptdl/ptdlib_1.html, which lists 80 PTDLs with corresponding hyperlinks to their Web sites. Approximately half of the PTDLs are academic, and the rest are public libraries. A PTDL is useful resource for general patent research and independent inventors.

Three PTDLs have resources that are similar in scope to the USPTO EAST system in Alexandria, Virginia. These libraries are known as "Partnership PTDLs" and are located in Sunnyvale, California, and College Station, Texas (north of Houston) and Detroit, Michigan. They provide general text and image searching, as does the EAST search system used by U.S. patent examiners.

Micropatent Patent Web

Micropatent PatentWeb is a fee-based, patent search engine. This Web-based system is easy to use and requires minimal training. As indicated in Exhibit 6.1, PatentWeb allows the user to query sections of a patent, in the patent databases of specific countries, within a defined number of years, excluding extraneous or known information. PatentWeb includes the full texts of patents and published applications granted by the U.S., EPO, PCT, DE, FR, JP, and GB. The system allows you to edit and "rerun" a search based on the resulting number of hits. Most helpful, PatentWeb permits the user save his or her search and return to it at another time.

The following exhibits show the progression of a search using MicroPatent PatentWeb. From the search history page (Exhibit. 6.1) to the

New Strategy | Saved Strategies | Alerts | Classes | Help

Temporary | AO neurotechnology | Automated Storage and ... | DkW - Dishwasher Sump | **JMG225** | IL 66771 | Presto (more)

	Save changes to current strategy	Save	Annotation
Save selected as		Save As
Append selected to	070605 ▼	Append
	☐ Delete this strategy	Delete

Add new search | Delete selected | Combine queries [ ] comment [ ] Combine

| ☑ # comments | results criteria | action last run |
| ☑ 1 | 272 hits | Full patent spec. ((microstrip or patch) near antenna) and ((dual or multiple) near5 (band or frequenc*3)) and (IEEE or 802.11) Databases USG USA Years 1836-2000 | rerun \| edit \| clone \| alert 2006-05-25 0 |

E X H I B I T   6 . 1   Search History Page

list of hits (Exhibit. 6.2), to finally the actual full text record (Exhibit. 6.4). The full-text record can also be downloaded as a PDF if desired.

Shown in the first figure, PatentWeb does not allow the searcher to search multiple sections of a patent at the same time. In other words, it is not possible to search for both "microfluidic" to be recited in the claims of a patent and "nucleic" to be recited in the specification. Although it will not perform this search in a single step, the user may achieve the same result using two steps: combining the results of each search and searching for their intersection.

In Exhibit 6.3, the one-page full-text patent with a .gif of the first figure is shown. Though this page allows a searcher to use the find command (Ctrl + F) to locate particular keywords within the text, a mechanical searcher has a difficult time with their search in the absence of figures. Also, it does take a few seconds for each full-text document to be loaded from a previous page. This is of minor concern with five patents, but when you need to review 100 patents, the amount of time spent becomes substantial.

Micropatent PatentWeb is exceptional in its ability to locate a U.S. patent's family members in the rest of the world (JP, DE, GB, EP, PCT, and FR at least). Typically, a mechanical patent granted in the United States can be found to have family members all over the world, such as Kampichler et al. (U.S. 6,446,542 B1), which is a novel piston and connecting rod assembly for an internal combustion engine. Using Patent-Web's family lookup feature, it was found that this particular patent has family members, or the same patent issued from four other patenting

Reference: JMG225
Search scope: US Granted US Applications; Full patent spec.
Years: 1836-2006
Text: ((microstrip or patch) near antenna) and ((dual or multiple) near5 (band or frequenc* 3)) and (IEEE or 802.11)

272 patents. This page is: 1 - 50 (Unsorted)

| Order/Download | Find Similar | [Choose an action!] | Go |

For additional processing options (graphs, sorting, reports), go to **WorkSheet**

Search History

☑ Highlight the search terms in the full-text record

Home   Search   First   Prev   Go to   Next   Last   Help

⦿ Check All   ⦿ Uncheck All

1. | US20060097894A1 | ☐ G08G 20060511 {n/a}
   Method and apparatus reporting a vehicular sensor waveform in a wireless vehicular sensor network
2. | US20060092079A1 | ☐ H01Q 20060504 {n/a}
   Ceramic antenna module and methods of manufacture thereof
3. | US20060089112A1 | ☐ H04B 20060427 {n/a}
   Wireless neural data acquisition system
4. | US20060084406A1 | ☐ H04B 20060420 {n/a}
   Systems and methods for increasing bandwidth of wireless communications
5. | US20060066496A1 | ☐ H01Q 20060330 Research In Motion Limited

E X H I B I T   6 . 2   **Search Hit List**

Home   Search   List   First   Prev   Go to   Next   Last   ☐ Include

MicroPatent® PatSearch Fulltext: Record 5 of 272

Reference: JMG225
Search scope: US Granted US Applications; Full patent spec.
Years: 1836-2006
Text: ((microstrip or patch) near antenna) and ((dual or multiple) near5 (band or frequenc*3)) and (IEEE or 802.11)

| Order/Download | Family Lookup | Find Similar | Legal Status |

Go to first matching text

US20060066496 A1
Multiple-band(^) antenna with shared slot structure
Research In Motion Limited

Abstract:
A <u>multiple-band(^)</u> antenna having first and second operating frequency bands is provided. The antenna includes a first patch structure associated primarily with the first operating frequency band, a second patch structure electrically coupled to the first patch structure and associated primarily with the second operating frequency band, a first slot structure disposed between a first portion of the first patch structure and the second patch structure and associated primarily with the first operating frequency band, and a second slot structure disposed between a second portion of the first patch

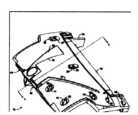

E X H I B I T   6 . 3   **Full Text Record**

authorities around the world. The downside to this feature is that the family lookup is an extra step, as the system does not automatically provide the family members linked to the subject "hit." Also, a patent family does not appear only once in a result set. Each member of the family appears as a single hit, making your number of result hits deceiving. It would be beneficial if each family member were a part of the same record and appeared only once in a result set, similar to that which is done in PatAnalyst.

A useful tool of many search engines is the option to search the patents cited on the face of a patent (backward citation) and to search the patents that cite your patent of interest (forward citation). This feature identifies similar patents and often reveals related classes and subclasses that may not have been searched. The different patent search engines accomplish citation searching differently. Micropatent PatentWeb shows abstract and bibliographic information after the user clicks on a red arrow citation link in a patent's full-text window. The full text of a cited patent can be viewed by simply clicking on one of a "full-text" navigation button near the top of the citation patent page. The system provides forward citation links, but the highlighting from the search terms does not carry through to the related patent, not originally selected.

Examiner Assisted Search Tool (EAST)

The EAST system is extraordinary. Unfortunately, EAST is accessible only at the USPTO campus in Alexandria, Virginia. The patent search system provides access to U.S. patent documents (published and granted), DWPI information, JPO data, IBM Technical Disclosure Bulletin (IBM_TDB), and EPO patent documents.

EAST may be searched using proximity operators and Boolean logic. Additionally, the system allows the user to search specific sections of multiple patent documents simultaneously, which is not possible in PatentWeb. For example, you could search for an inventor by entering ".*IN.*" following his last name; you could search for a specific word to appear in the title by entering ".*TI.*" following your search terms. Exhibit 6.4 displays the searchable fields in EAST.

As can be seen in Exhibit 6.4, EAST allows users to view data in three panes. You may view the patent image, the history of your search, and a list of search hits concurrently. The user may even view sections of patents

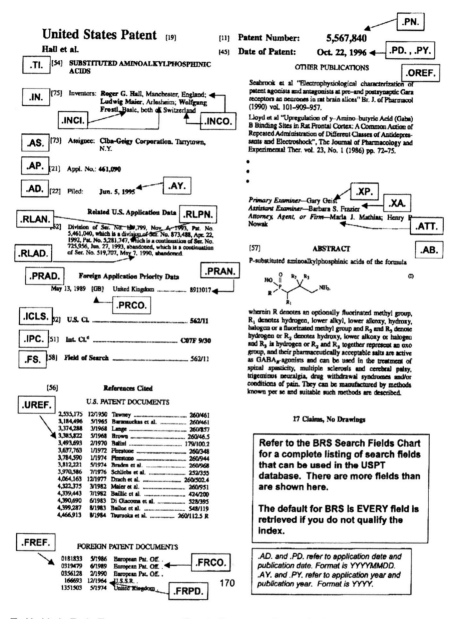

.PN.

United States Patent [19]

Hall et al.

[11] Patent Number: **5,567,840**

[45] Date of Patent: Oct. 22, 1996 ◄ .PD., .PY.

.TI. [54] SUBSTITUTED AMINOALKYLPHOSPHINIC ACIDS

.OREF.

OTHER PUBLICATIONS

Seabrook et al "Electrophysiological characterization of patent agonists and antagonists at pre- and postsynaptic Gaba receptors an neurones in rat brain slices" Br. J. of Pharmacol (1990) vol. 101-909-957.

Lloyd et al "Upregulation of y-Amino-butyric Acid (Gaba) B Binding Sites in Rat Frontal Cortex; A Common Action of Repeated Administration of Different Classes of Antidepressants and Electroshock", The Journal of Pharmacology and Experimental Ther. vol. 23, No. 1 (1986) pp. 72-75.

.IN. [75] Inventors: Roger G. Hall, Manchester, England; Ludwig Maier, Arlesheim; Wolfgang Frostl, Basle, both of Switzerland

.INCI.

.INCO.

.AS. [73] Assignee: Ciba-Geigy Corporation, Tarrytown, N.Y.

.AP. [21] Appl. No.: 461,090

.AD. [22] Filed: Jun. 5, 1995 .AY.

.XP.

Primary Examiner—Gary Geist
Assistant Examiner—Barbara S. Frazier .XA.
Attorney, Agent, or Firm—Marla J. Mathias; Henry P Nowak

.ATT.

Related U.S. Application Data .RLPN.

.RLAN.

[62] Division of Ser. No. 189,799, Nov. 4, 1993, Pat. No. 5,461,040, which is a division of Ser. No. 873,488, Apr. 22, 1992, Pat. No. 5,281,747, which is a continuation of Ser. No. 725,956, Jun. 27, 1993, abandoned, which is a continuation of Ser. No. 519,707, May 7, 1990, abandoned.

.RLAD.

[57] ABSTRACT .AB.

P-substituted aminoalkylphosphinic acids of the formula

.PRAD. Foreign Application Priority Data .PRAN.

May 13, 1989 [GB] United Kingdom 8911017

.PRCO.

.ICLS. [52] U.S. Cl. 562/11

.IPC. [51] Int. Cl.⁶ C07F 9/30

.FS. [58] Field of Search 562/11

$$HO - \underset{R}{\overset{O}{\underset{|}{P}}} - \underset{R_1}{\overset{R_2\ R_3}{C}} - NH_2,$$ (1)

wherein R denotes an optionally fluorinated methyl group, R_1 denotes hydrogen, lower alkyl, lower alkoxy, hydroxy, halogen or a fluorinated methyl group and R_2 and R_3 denote hydrogen or R_2 denotes hydroxy, lower alkoxy or halogen and R_3 is hydrogen or R_2 and R_3 together represent an oxo group, and their pharmaceutically acceptable salts are active as GABA$_B$-agonists and can be used in the treatment of spinal spasticity, multiple sclerosis and cerebral palsy, trigeminus neuralgia, drug withdrawal syndromes and/or conditions of pain. They can be manufactured by methods known per se and suitable such methods are described.

[56] References Cited

.UREF.

U.S. PATENT DOCUMENTS

2,535,175	12/1950	Tawney	260/461
3,184,496	5/1965	Baranauckas et al.	260/461
3,374,288	3/1968	Lange	260/357
3,385,822	5/1968	Brown	260/46.5
3,493,693	2/1970	Balini	179/100.2
3,637,763	1/1972	Firestone	260/348
3,784,590	1/1974	Firestone	260/944
3,812,221	5/1974	Braden et al.	260/968
3,970,586	7/1976	Schliebs et al.	252/355
4,064,163	12/1977	Drach et al.	260/502.4
4,322,375	3/1982	Maier et al.	260/951
4,339,443	7/1982	Baillie et al.	424/200
4,390,690	6/1983	Di Giacoma et al.	528/395
4,399,287	8/1983	Bailoe et al.	548/119
4,466,913	8/1984	Tsuruoka et al.	260/112.5 R

17 Claims, No Drawings

Refer to the BRS Search Fields Chart for a complete listing of search fields that can be used in the USPT database. There are more fields than are shown here.

The default for BRS is EVERY field is retrieved if you do not qualify the index.

.FREF.

FOREIGN PATENT DOCUMENTS

0181833	5/1986	European Pat. Off.	
0319479	6/1989	European Pat. Off.	.FRCO.
0356128	2/1990	European Pat. Off.	
166693	12/1964	U.S.S.R.	
1351503	5/1974	United Kingdom	.FRPD.

170

.AD. and .PD. refer to application date and publication date. Format is YYYYMMDD.
.AY. and .PY. refer to application year and publication year. Format is YYYY.

E X H I B I T   6 . 4   **East System Search Operators**

during the search (i.e., only the drawings or figures from one patent to another without having to review patent text). This feature permits expeditious searches of mechanical art. Finally, the full images of patents are loaded immediately to the user, which greatly reduces the time required to otherwise load images from competing search engines during a search.

EAST includes DWPI records, which permit the user to search patent family records. EAST also highlights entered search terms in the results. For example, in the top left pane of Exhibit 6.5, the "text" tab is selected and includes highlighted "arrays," "Gingeras," and "Affymetrix." This word, the inventor, and the assignee were entered as search terms and then subsequently highlighted in the result. This is very helpful when a large patent is being examined and the relevant sections need to be understood.

Thomson Delphion

Delphion provides access to U.S., European, and German granted patents and published applications. The search system also provides access to

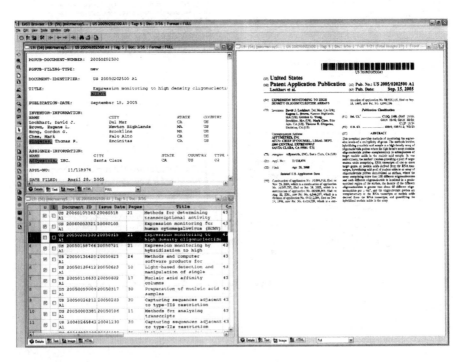

E X H I B I T   6 . 5   **East System Search Panes**

DWPI, INPADOC, Japanese Abstracts, Swiss granted patents, and WIPO PCT published applications. Delphion is unusual in that provides more than patent document coverage—it provides access to some NPL.

Delphion has some tools for creating patent maps and charts and, when offline, allows the user to save files, organize, annotate, and share personalized lists of patents. The search system supports bulk downloads of patents and fast export of bibliographic fields. Although there has been some acceptance of Delphion by professional searchers, many of its users are company engineers and independent inventors.

Questel-Orbit

Questel-Orbit has several databases. Some of them are "pay as you go," while others may be obtained through subscription. The coverage differs for each patent authority, so it is important to review the database coverage, as with any provider. You can find Questel-Orbit data coverage at www.questel.orbit.com/EN/Prodsandservices/patents_search.htm.

There are more than 100 databases offered by Questel-Orbit, but some more than others have features that are available for specific user needs. For example, the DWPI First View offers English-language abstracts for Chinese, Japanese, Korean, Taiwanese, and Russian patents. Also, Litigation Alert (LITA) is available, which gives litigation coverage from 1970 to the present of patent and trademark infringement lawsuits reported to the Patent and Trademark Commission. Other all-encompassing databases for patents and nonpatent publications are available that allow a user to search the French Patent Office, EPO, WIPO, and the USPTO.

QPAT, a patent search system, can be subscribed to daily, weekly, monthly, or annually, and can cover one or all of the previously stated authorities as well as FamPat, which is Questel-Orbit's international patent file. FamPat is organized by families from over 75 patenting authorities and allows a user to view abstracts of family members in English, while the full text is available in the original language along with legal status.

PatAnalyst

PatAnalyst is similar to EAST in its coverage and was built for the EPO examining corps. However, the search system is relatively expensive and has some shortcomings. For example, when searching in either EAST or PatentWeb, the queried search term appears highlighted throughout the text of all search results. This is not true for PatAnalyst (see Exhibit 6.6). Instead, the data is visualized in the manner below. In essence, the power of seeing highlighted terms in proximity to one another (as the syntax required in the original query) is lost. Additionally, this is another step that has to be taken before reviewing the results of a search query and increases the time it takes to find a reference.

Another downside to the system is its lack of forward and backward citation links. Unlike other tools, such as PatentWeb, which allows the user to concurrently download many PDF images of a patent, PatAnalyst allows the searcher to order only one PDF version of a patent at a time. Bulk patent downloading saves time and avoids the need to enter every patent number separately and wait for each to download.

PatAnalyst's primary strength is its ability to view all images of a patent and the automatically present family groupings. This is an exceptional strength of the system. As can be seen in Exhibit 6.7, the full image is available to the searcher, as are the family members (in this case only one French patent).

Click on the Pen icons ✐ to define expressions to be highlighted in your documents.

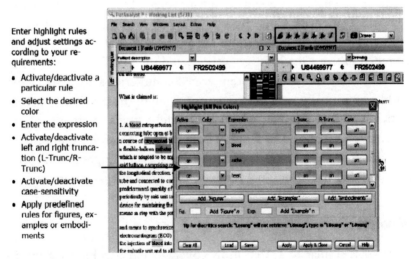

Enter highlight rules and adjust settings according to your requirements:

- Activate/deactivate a particular rule
- Select the desired color
- Enter the expression
- Activate/deactivate left and right truncation (L-Trunc/R-Trunc)
- Activate/deactivate case-sensitivity
- Apply predefined rules for figures, examples or embodiments

E X H I B I T   6 . 6   **Patanalyst**

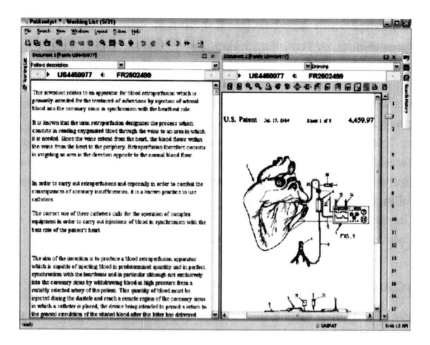

EXHIBIT 6.7   PatAnalyst Panes

Minesoft PatBase

PatBase is a Web-based application that was developed by searchers to provide a streamlined, customizable search program. It reportedly has access to 28 million patent families. Like some other commercially available software, PatBase provides full-text and classification searching, citation searching, statistical analysis tools, and results folders.

The most obvious distinction of PatBase compared to its competitors is its customization. Every feature of PatBase can be customized to fit an individual searcher's needs based on preference or on the type of search being performed. For example, if a searcher is looking for a mechanical device that requires a review of the drawings of a patent, a classic view can be used displaying the abstract and a graphic that acts as a link to all of the patent's drawings provided by the EPO's Web site. If a clearance search is being conducted, a view with a patent's claims can be chosen to determine the scope of protection.

Another key feature of PatBase is displaying results grouped by patent family, which consolidates related patents into a single record, with links to the individual family members (see Exhibit 6.8). This allows for more efficient searching by removing redundant results while providing a list of the oldest and newest patent documents in a family, which may be important in searches that rely on date-specific results.

In addition, PatBase also offers statistical analysis of the most prevalent assignees and classifications of a particular search query. In figure "M," the query "piston and engine and (internal combustion)" was entered into the command line. The resulting graph shows where the 500 most recent patents were classified in the U.S. classification system. This feature proves useful in analytic approaches.

The streamlined searching, access to all of a patent's images, and customization make PatBase an attractive patent database tool.

ACCESS TO NONPATENT LITERATURE

Insight into existing inventions can offer hope for other inventions in production by offering new ways to solve problems that may not have previously existed and may never have come to light had the application not

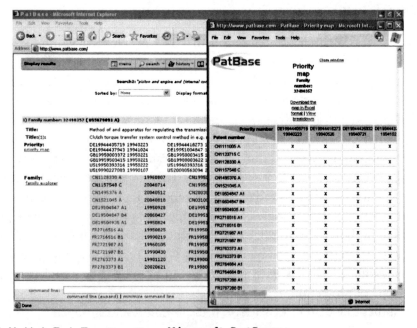

E X H I B I T   6 . 8   Minesoft PatBase

been submitted. As an applicant or inventor beginning the search through what tops seven million U.S. patents to date, this can be an enormous task, the difficulty of which is compounded by the existing NPL on which this section will focus. This section will inform you how to approach your search for nonpatent written material (articles, technical publications, advertising, dissertations, etc.).

Each of the NPL providers house many different files, each including many relevant journals, scientific conference abstracts, doctoral theses, and the like related to a particular subject matter. In addition, IP.com's prior art database is home to a wide array of technical disclosures from many *Fortune* 500 companies. In addition to the anonymous publications by many prominent companies, you will also find disclosures published with full authorship information from innovative companies such as IBM, Motorola, and Siemens. The IP.com Prior Art Database is also the exclusive location for new IBM Technical Disclosure Bulletin (TDB) documents on the Web.[17] As such, an IP.com search may prove helpful in a mechanical or EE-based search, among others (see Exhibit 6.9).

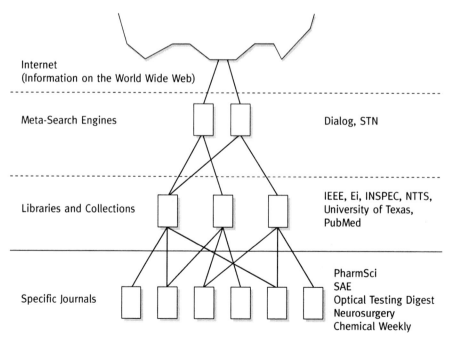

Internet
(Information on the World Wide Web)

Meta-Search Engines   Dialog, STN

Libraries and Collections   IEEE, Ei, INSPEC, NTTS, University of Texas, PubMed

Specific Journals   PharmSci SAE Optical Testing Digest Neurosurgery Chemical Weekly

E X H I B I T 6 . 9 **General and Specific Search Tools**

One difficulty of searching technical publications is that the underlying articles are not always publicly available. Sometimes the publisher's copyright fee is cost prohibitive if you need to survey many full text articles. Subscriptions to different data repositories such as those offered by ProQuest, Reed Elsevier, EBSCO, or to individual journals themselves may be cost effective in the long run.

Some search engines, such as Delphion (see Exhibit 6.10), cover both patent and nonpatent literature. However, Delphion draws its information directly from other sources, namely IP.com and IBM TDB. After a search is entered, only the abstract is available from IP.com unless the searcher also holds a subscription to IP.com. Fortunately, the NPL from the IBM TDB is available in full, though as might have been surmised, the NPL scope of Delphion reaches primarily into the high-tech realm of electronics and computers.

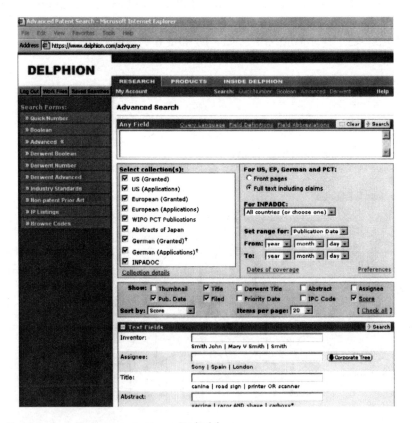

E X H I B I T   6 . 1 0   **Delphion**

The Internet   There are millions of definitions for the Internet, and even more variations on how large it is. However, generalizations can be made and those numbers can at times be far larger than we ever may have imagined. Although no one person can tell you the exact size of the World Wide Web, it can in fact be managed and searched with patience and knowledge.

If it exists, there is probably a reference to it somewhere on the Web. There are both benefits and pitfalls to this sort of access. Some of the benefits include the ease of finding information—you don't even have to move from your plush leather computer chair to have the world at your fingertips. It is open 24 hours a day, 365 days a year, which means you can surf for information anytime day or night. There are no limits to how much data you can find. Some of the pitfalls are that not all data on the Web is legitimate. Some of the data is based on half truths and some is outright false.

Dates are hard to find. Because Web pages are constantly updated, an idea that may have existed for years cannot be considered prior art simply because no public release date exists. Reputable sources are hard to find, and an estimated 40 million Web pages are thought to exist. The world's most renowned bean sprout farmer may have a home page listed with his bug-resistant variety of bean sprout and how he genetically altered this gene through several experimental hybridizations. This information obviously is in existence and made available to the public. However, it may need to be ignored if the date cannot be verified. Although this lacks our requirement for good steadfast prior art, it may lead you to information that is well documented. So the grain-of-salt reference may actually be a gem once it is explored thoroughly.

So you have reached the Internet and you need to begin to search through the massive superhighway of information that exists in front of you. Where do you begin? Perhaps you might start by typing keywords into Google (www.google.com).

Google is the Internet's most popular search engine at the time this text was written, with over 50 percent of search engine market share. It is an excellent choice but by no means perfect. Google runs on a distributed network of thousands of computers that are capable of rapid parallel processing. Parallel processing is simply the simultaneous use of more than one central processing unit (CPU) to execute a program—a method that can significantly speed up data processing.

Google has three distinct parts, including a "Googlebot" (a Web crawler that finds and fetches Web pages), an "Indexer" (which is capable of sorting every word on every page and storing the results in a database), and the "Query Processor" (which compares your typed search text to the database and provides an indication of relevancy. We will take a closer at each part and discuss how it relates to the NPL that we seek.

Googlebot is a robot of sorts that browses the Web constantly and retrieves pages, which are turned over to the indexer. Some people have described the Web as a vast spider web of random Web sites all linked together, and the Googlebot as a spider working its way across the Web and collecting information, but in reality Googlebot does not traverse the Web; it actually sends a request to a Web server for a Web page and then proceeds to download the entire page, which it passes along to the indexer. Googlebot is highly efficient and especially effective for information that remains the same over a period of time. In essence, what you are searching is in the past, so therefore you may come across data that no longer exists or is outdated. Also, the spider we spoke of may not have yet crawled far enough to reach a particular page yet, which is why the date on which the page is indexed is also crucial. Each of these could be crucial to the overall efficacy of a search and is a reason that searchers using Google should use other sources as well.

The indexer stores pages received from the Googlebot in Google's index database. This index is sorted alphabetically by search term, which allows rapid access to documents that contain user query terms. To speed things up, common words are not indexed. These are referred to as *stop words*. Examples include is, on, or, of, how, and why.

The indexer could not function without the query processor, which can evaluate the search string that you input and match it to relevant documents. Google's priority has several factors that will not be discussed; however, Google gives more priority to pages that have search terms near each other and in the same order as the query.

Since Google indexes hypertext markup language (HTML) code in addition to the text on the page, users can restrict searches on the basis of where query words appear (e.g., in the title, in the URL, in the body, and in links to the page—options offered by the Advanced-Search page and search operators).

The Internet Needs a Skilled Searcher The Internet has vast amount of information that is useful only to those who can separate the trash from the treasure. It is full of unorganized information and misinformation, much of which is difficult to sort through.

Google is a powerful tool. However, general search engines are only as good as the skill of the person using them. For example, an unskilled searcher might enter the term *battery pack* in Google. He would retrieve 39 million results, most heavily skewed toward stores that sell battery packs. These are too many records to be useful. The skilled searcher would first ask himself critical questions to hone the search further. He might ask, "What is a battery pack? What is it made up of? Can it be separated into smaller parts? What about a portable power cell? What about an auxiliary power source?" In doing so, the experienced searcher will return better, more manageable results.

Meta-Search Engines A meta-search engine searches several other databases and search engines simultaneously and returns results from each one. It is nearly impossible to catalog the entire Web, so the theory here is that by searching multiple search engines you are able to search more of the Web in less time.

Meta-search engines' popularity has increased in recent years, mainly due to the ease of use and high probability of finding the desired results. The flaw in these engines lies in the exorbitant number of extraneous matches that result from any given search. This is usually outweighed in those searches wherein results are far too few by giving the user obscure data that may not have been found while using a single engine. There are many meta-searches available on the Web, and each differs in the results it gives back and the sources it uses for data. Meta-searches are becoming more popular as people look for more powerful results in less time.

DialogWeb Specialized meta-engines are also finding a niche in the world of NPL searches. One such engine is named DialogWeb (www.dialog.com). DialogWeb provides easy access to the full content (over 600 databases), power, and precision of classic Dialog through a Web browser. This service caters to those in the business of intellectual property (IP) as well as small organizations. Even though most of the information Dialog accesses is public information and accessible for free, DialogWeb gives the user the access to these sources without having to visit each site individually all in one easy-to-use Web application.

IP.com IP.com (www.ip.com) goes a step further, adding several powerful tools for searching nonpatent prior art. These tools do come at a cost, currently starting at $300 per week for an individual subscription. In return, you receive access to a company database that is ever changing.

The IP.com Prior Art Database is a unique database dedicated to the publication of technical disclosure documents. Its sole purpose is to enable the creation of and access to prior art. The IP.com Prior Art Database contains content exclusive to IP.com, and is an essential source of NPL for IP professionals, research and development (R&D) staff, corporate library staff, and individual inventors.

The database itself contains a wide array of technical disclosures from many companies. In addition to the anonymous publications by prominent companies, you will also find disclosures published with full authorship information from innovative companies such as IBM, Motorola, and Siemens.

Much of the content in the IP.com Prior Art Database cannot be found anywhere else in the world. The IP.com Prior Art Database content is published intentionally and specifically to create formal prior art. Each disclosure is digitally notarized upon publication in order to guarantee that the content and date are firmly established in the public domain. Some companies use the IP.com Prior Art Database as their sole channel for putting innovation into the public domain.

IEEE Xplore IEEE Xplore (http://ieeexplore.ieee.org) is an online delivery system providing full-text access to the world's highest-quality technical literature in electrical engineering, computer science, and electronics. IEEE Xplore contains full-text documents from IEEE journals, transactions, magazines, letters, conference proceedings, standards, and IEE (Institution of Electrical Engineers) publications. It currently covers over one million documents, so it is well worth the subscription fee if your searches focus on engineering. It also has features you can access for free, such as a list of the top 100 most accessed articles, which can give interesting insight into where current research is heading.

Meta-search engines provide easy access to a variety of technical journals as well. Most universities have their own library meta-search engine, which can be an invaluable tool if you have access. Others prefer third-party systems such as Science Direct (www.sciencedirect.com), which claims to be the world's largest electronic collection of science, technology, and medicine full-text and bibliographic information. It allows full-text searching for subscribers of a large amount of biotechnology and medical journals with an easy-to-use interface. It also allows for alerts customized to your research so you can get up-to-the-minute publications without having to retype search queries. Although generally individual journals can be accessed on a pay-per-view basis, searching each journal's site can be tedious and time consuming.

NCBI   The National Center for Biotechnology Information (NCBI) was established in 1988 as a national resource for molecular biology information; NCBI creates public databases, conducts research in computational biology, develops software tools for analyzing genome data, and disseminates biomedical information.

The strength of NCBI's databases are its highly organized and comprehensive information that allows you to search genetic sequence databases by way of GenBank. You could search literature using PubMed, which at press contained over 15 million citations. The resources on this site are too numerous to mention and are constantly updated. They should be consulted by anyone who is searching in the field of biotechnology or medicine.

Science and Technology/Chemical Abstracts Services (STN/CAS) (www.cas.org) connects scientists, engineers, and anyone who needs technical information to the world's most complete and authoritative databases. You can identify public patents and published research in all scientific fields, as well as search chemical substance information by name, structure, or CAS registry number. This provides another powerful tool that combines multiple sources in one easy-to-use Web-based service, albeit at a premium.

Searching Journals   Finding technical publications is not difficult. Sorting through the information to find what is reliable and what is relevant, however, can be time consuming and frustrating. Thus, if you have already conducted a search of patents, you might make an interesting observation: that many patents cite technical literature.

In fast-emerging fields like biotechnology, there often exists more nonpatent than patent literature. A study published in 1996 of citation analyses disclosed that as few as 150 journals account for half of what is cited and one quarter of what is published. It has also been shown that a core of approximately 2,000 journals accounts for about 85 percent of published articles and 95 percent of cited articles.[18]

In other words, if you can focus on the publications that are most often cited on patents of similar technologies, you can find articles that would likely have relevance to your subject matter in the time allotted for the completion of the search.

Reviewing EPOQUE data from 1990 through 1999, it was discovered that an average of three NPL citations were used by the USPTO for each application received.[19]

We can presume that fast-developing areas such as biotechnology will result in more nonpatent citations than, say, an invention for an eating utensil. The mere fact that all of the applications combined tallied an average of three citations per application shows how a search outside patent literature is necessary.

The published journal articles show how the invention was developed and act as a dated stamp for the inventor. However, the rights are usually owned by the organization that issues the grant, and most financial gains resulting from its use and sale are also inherently owned by the organizations.

Specifically targeting scientific research one might have a National Institutes of Health (NIH) or a National Science Foundation (NSF)–based grant. If a project submitted under that grant results in the finding of a novel enzyme, it may be marketed for profit. The burden falls on the NIH or NSF and the organization or university for whom the inventor is employed to patent the enzyme. The journal publication first authored by the inventors is what was ultimately sought after from the beginning.

Conference Proceedings   Conference databases offer ever-changing, up-to-date information on specific topics. Many of the meta-search engines discussed previously include these references in their results. Conferences are full of speeches, presentations, and written opinions; these are meetings of the minds in a specialized subject area. With many conferences, the full texts of the proceeding are available online. Some are in the form of abstracts, but nevertheless they can be useful.

Scientists, in particular, tend to over speak at conferences. This means that you may learn of their disclosure even before the publication is printed. We have found conference proceedings to be particularly useful when conducting validity searches.

Newspapers, Magazines, and Catalogues   You pick up a newspaper and read through the pages. You may not realize that newspapers are an excellent resource of prior art. Moreover, newspapers have verifiable publicly available dates.

Their shortfall, however, is that newspapers and magazines often lack detailed discussions. When disclosed, many newspapers will name the invention and what it does, but not how it works. With respect to a prior art search, the mere fact that a device that can pick cherries from a tree is not as important as its mechanical aspects.

You occasionally can use newspapers and magazines to assist with the date of publication. For example, if you have the specifications of an invention but no date of its disclosure, you can search for the date in which it was sold or announced to the public generally. Catalogs often have a month and year date on them. You can easily find out when newspapers and magazines have reached the public. Then, merely combine the specifications with the date and share the two with legal counsel.

VALUE-ADDED CAPABILITIES OF SEARCH TOOLS

Each patent search engine or NPL data provider has subtle difference in the way the approach search their respective resources. Search engines offer different capabilities. The more basic capabilities are inherent to the engine, such as text query complexity, database coverage, viewing capacity, and accessibility. The extra capabilities are those that enhance the users' ability to quickly and easily gather their required information. Without some of the extra capabilities, the users may omit information crucial to the end product. While the amounts of features offered are numerous, presenting those features that reliably aid in supplementing a searcher's work follows.

Alerting

While searches are generally performed once, it is occasionally necessary to "rerun" a search at regular intervals (possible per quarter, annually, or weekly). Alternatively, a particular searched subject matter may frequently require a search. Instead of repeating the same query multiple times, you can save resources by setting an "alerting" mechanism within the search engine itself to carry out the search again at an assigned time. The feature provides not only for work to get done, without actually doing it yourself, but also it provides an alarm or reminder ensuring a thorough search of the subject matter. Alerting is useful for staying current with fast-moving technologies.

Search History

Search histories are crucial portions of a searcher's final product. A well-organized search history will disclose the search's entire set of keywords and logical operators that were used. At other times, the search history can simply be used as a record to reduce redundancy in subsequent searching.

Depending on the search engine, the search history may be only the record of what was searched. Some systems offer only the syntax of what has been searched before, while others allow the user to analyze a number of search queries and combine them to find unions, edit, or copy existing queries, and mark or flag queries in the history for organizational purposes.

Information and Image Importing and Exporting

Exporting information from a search engine to a report or document is a feature that not only adds merit for the substantiation of a search, but offers a glimpse into that which the searcher was thinking at the time of the query. Some tools (e.g., EAST) are very restrictive.

Micropatent PatentWeb offers an option wherein patent numbers can be imported into a dialog box and the program submits a spreadsheet with every piece of pertinent information from the title and inventor to the claims of the patent in Spanish. This ability to organize your data prior to analysis is a time saver.

The ability to export images is sometimes as important as exporting data. The drawings are the most useful parts of a mechanical patent. The best search engines allow the user to import and export images and underlying text in a number of file formats that can be viewed in various programs.

Legal Status, Maintenance Fees, and Prosecution

The legal status of a patent is important when conducting infringement or validity searches. INPADOC (INPD) has the legal status of patent documents in 50 countries. Search tools like Delphion and Questel/Orbit provide access to INPD. The USPTO Web portal known as PAIR, found at http://portal.uspto.gov/external/portal/pair, provides U.S. patent application data, transaction history, and fees.

Costs

An expensive search engine is not necessarily a quality tool. The variety of available search engines and data providers makes selecting the most appropriate one somewhat daunting. Each patent search engine has different data coverage, different access points (single user vs. multiuser flat fee), varying data retrieval methods and speeds, and added capabilities, as previously discussed. Similarly, data providers have different hourly access fees to particular files, different display charges, various specialty search charges, and many ways in which to access full-text articles.

Most search tools may be tested for free for a trial period. This testing period is a perfect way to answer a user's questions with regard to the system's capabilities and whether or not it is worth the price. The amount of usage is also a difficult variable to predict when shopping for search engines. Most likely, the usage amount dictates how much the subscription will cost and the trial period is helpful in estimating potential usage. Single-user subscriptions can be obtained that, while cheaper than a multi-user account, may not provide unlimited searching. Therefore, a less expensive initial investment may prove more expensive in the long run. For instance, one search engine provider may offer its engine for $8,000 a year per user, but another company may offer its engine for $50,000 a year with an unlimited amount of logons by an unlimited amount of users.

Visualization

The ability to query different parts of a patent is crucial to a search. There are many patent search tools that allow the review of patent images and parts of a patent (i.e., specification, claims, drawings, etc.), each with strengths and weaknesses.

CONCLUSION

The value of a patent search engine depends on the user, as each user's needs will dictate his or her selection. Fully investigating the available options and testing each engine through trials will provide you with the choice that fits your needs.

NOTES

1. The reader is encouraged to monitor the Patent Users Information Group (PIUG) Discussion List for new enhancements to patent search engines and patent data sources. The discussion list is free and contains a treasure of information about where and how to access patent information. Visit www.piug.org on the Internet.
2. http://stneasy.cas.org/dbss/help.REGISTRY.html.
3. www.ncbi.nih.gov/.
4. www.uspto.gov/web/patents/searchtemplates/class530-331.htm.
5. www.stn-international.com/archive/pressroom/pressreleases/USGENE_en.html.
6. "The current patent numbering system began with a patent issued on July 13, 1836. Prior to that date, 9,957 patents had been issued" (www.uspto.gov/go/taf/issuyear.htm).
7. www.delphion.com/collect_descrip.
8. "There were a total of 2,845 patents restored from the fire, most of which were eventually given a number beginning with "X." All patents after the date of the establishment of the Patent Office in July 1836 were numbered as a new series (without the X), beginning with a new Patent No. 1 to John Ruggles." (www.uspto.gov/web/offices/ac/ahrpa/opa/kids/special/1836fire.htm).
9. www.ei.org/compendex.html.
10. www.ei.org/ntis.html.
11. The Institution of Engineering and Technology was recently formed by the joining of The Institution of Electrical Engineers (IEE) and The Institution of Incorporated Engineers.
12. www.iee.org/publish/inspec/.
13. www.ieee.org/products/onlinepubs/prod/iel_overview.html.
14. *State Street Bank & Trust Co. v. Signal Financial Group, Inc.* 149 F.3d 1368 (Fed. Cir. 1998) *cert. denied*, 119 S. Ct. 851 (1999).
15. www.uspto.gov/web/menu/pbmethod/aiplafall02paper.htm.
16. www.sec.gov/edgar.shtml.
17. www.ip.com/pad/priorArtDatabase.jsp?id=search.
18. Garfield, E., The Significant Scientific Literature Appears in a Small Core of Journals. *The Scientist*, Vol. 10, No. 17, September 2, 1996.
19. Jacques Michel, B.B., Patent Citation Analysis, *Scientometrics*, Vol. 51, No. 1, 2001: pp. 185–201.

Index

Patent applications. *See* Application for
  patent
Patent Café ICO Suite, 146
Patent Cooperation Treaty (PCT), 5, 75,
  77–80, 89
  search report, 16
  searches, 18, 26, 161, 162, 167
Patent examination, 13–17. *See also* Patent
  prosecution
Patent examiners, 12–18, 45, 46, 143,
  161
Patent landscape searches, 31, 32, 74, 146
Patent law, sources of, 2, 4–6, 12
Patent prosecution, 2, 11–17
Patent term, 5
Patentability search, 21–23, 60, 61, 138
PatentWeb, 146, 147, 154, 160–164, 168,
  180
Patolis, 156
pdf files, 147, 159, 162, 168
PIR, 152
Plant patent, 6
Prior art, 6, 83. *See also* References (prior
  art)
Priority date, 5–7, 52, 78, 83, 137
Problem-solution approach, 37–41
ProQuest, 172
Proximity operators, 48–51, 81, 82, 159,
  164
PubMed, 86, 171, 177

Questel-Orbit, 181
  FamPat, 167
  QPAT, 146, 167
  QWEB, 146

Reed Elsevier, 172
Reexam proceedings, 17
References (prior art), 6
  applicant's search, 15, 16
  applied to claims of applicant, 17
  approaches to search, 16
  benefits of searches, 32, 33
  central, 138, 140, 141
  disclosure of, 15
  discussion of in report, 132–136
  and invalidation of granted patent, 23
  list of cited references, 8
  and patent file history, 8
  and patentability search, 21

peripheral, 139–141
prioritizing for report, 137–141
searches versus analysis, 110, 111
summary chart, 133
and validity searches, 24
Reissue proceedings, 17
Rejections, 13, 15, 16, 60, 73, 83, 84
Relevance, screening for, 35, 43, 45,
  52–62, 64, 65, 67, 72–74, 80, 95,
  101, 174, 177
Reports
  approach, 128, 129
  claims information, 136, 137
  classification areas searched, 142
  contents of, 127–129
  databases searched, 143
  examiners contacted, 143
  exporting information to, 180
  feature matrix, use of, 59
  format, 129
  patent analysis, 112–125
  purpose of, 127, 128
  references, 62, 132–141
  search history, 141–144
  search results, order of, 62
  subject features, 130–132
  summary, 129, 130
Research and development (R&D), 3, 4,
  110, 176
Restriction requirement, 13
Right-to-use searches. *See* Clearance
  searches

Science and Technology/Chemical
  Abstracts Services (STN/CAS), 177
Science and Technology (STN), 87–91,
  152, 153, 160, 171, 177
Science Direct, 86, 177
Search engines. *See also* Databases
  citation searching, 72, 101, 164.
    See also Citation searches
  data coverage, 151
  drawings, 105
  foreign patents, 82
  Google. *See* Google
  keywords. *See* Keywords
  meta-search, 157, 175, 176, 178
  nonpatent literature, 83, 87, 172
  resources, 146
  search operators, 48–51, 159, 160

Lightning Source UK Ltd.
Milton Keynes UK
UKOW05n2147190814

237187UK00001B/8/P